The Slimshanks Chronicle

The Slimshanks Chronicle

Tales of Travel Travail and Escapade

Bob Machin

Burlington, Vermont

None of the names herein have been changed to protect the guilty and none of these stories is fiction. They find Slimshanks in various places around the globe caught in situations that range from the miraculous and terrifying to the absurd. Many take place in Latin America among indigenous and campesino cultures. Others ricochet between a wayward dog, a suicidal truck and the algebra between sex and lunch.

Onion River Press
191 Bank Street
Burlington, VT 05401

ISBN: 978-1-949066-52-4

To all adventurous souls.

Thanks to my sister Gale Machin who did the hard work wrestling these tales into shape. And thanks to Rachel Fisher at Onion River for going beyond the call of duty to create a real book.

Contents

{ vii }

Contents

MOTORING WITH THE DEVIL

Some thrills are cheaper than others. Cheaper out of pocket, like plunking down a dollar to ride the roller coaster or peeking under the circus tent to watch the bald-headed lady put on her wig. Or cheaper when it comes to putting your life on the line. Who is to draw up the percentages between racing that freight to the next crossing versus jumping out of a plane at 10,000 feet? People die every year looking for cheap thrills and finding danger. The more dangerous the adventure the more thrill potential it holds, but there is no telling in advance whether you'll beat that train to the crossing or become carnage in the attempt. You can race cars or ride bulls or climb vertical mountain walls or ride to the mountain top in a gondola and end up broken on the way down.

Most of these thrills and accompanying danger are more attractive to young people and, overwhelmingly, young male people. Older and wiser takes on great significance in this discussion. Young male people will do extraordinarily stupid things in their yearning for ever more expensive thrills. This syndrome might lead one from riding downhill on the handlebars of his bicycle to attacking the racetrack with some raging behemoth of an autocar that he has engineered. One of the more typical way stations for young males on their journey to older and wiser is a motorcycle. Motorcycles, when first acquired, are not perceived by their young pilots as dangerous, but the thrill factor is with them from the beginning. Speed, wind in your face, the siren song of the open road – the romance of the modern cowboy has replaced the horse with a motorcycle and the chance of death by .45 with the infinitely greater chance of death by speed, wind or the sirens.

It is spectacularly easy to die riding a motorcycle. It happens to young men all the time but Slimshanks never gave it a second thought when he felt the urge and bought himself a brand new bike. He had finagled a summer job in the Netherlands and figured he could skip a weekend over and back to London and pick up a Triumph. When you conjure a picture in your mind of a classic motorcycle, you are imaging the profile of a Triumph Bonneville or perhaps its cousin, the Norton Commando. These are English bikes and it was a Triumph that Lawrence of Arabia careened off the road to his death. Slim didn't think about the careening part, just that if it were good enough for Lawrence it would be the one for him. These classic English bikes didn't exhibit the brute and heavy power of a Harley or the pragmatic ungainliness of a BMW but hearken to the original American classic, the Indian. It was sleek and chromed, a young man's delight, and brutal to the extent that it would outclock just about any car to 60 mph. It was thrilling and it was deadly.

Slim was sharing the cost with a friend and it was his to purchase and ride to a reunion point in Sweden where he would hand it over and the friend would arrange its passage back to the U.S. The Triumph man at the factory, in that supercilious English way, was reluctant to let the bike go with Slim's choice of American handlebars. Slim didn't feature the prospect of cruising the highway for hours crouching bent over the stubby racing handlebars that was part of the 'real' Triumph package. He made it out of London unscathed but before he even reached the English Channel he had his first brush with death.

A certain mindset comes over a motorcycle rider somewhat like the worm that invades the brain of a moose and which leads the moose to shed his habitual wariness and the rider to proceed with disdain around and through slow moving automotive dinosaurs. Slim was not immune to the effects of this worm and as he cycled toward the coast at Dover he came up on a large panel truck inching along. Not to be deterred by this lumbering impediment, he quickly cut to the outside edge without slowing down and found himself staring into the wide eyes of two guys with picks and shovels excavating behind a wooden barrier. The near man abandoned his tools and jumped for his life, landing on top of the far man and Slim closed his eyes so as not to witness his own destruction and aimed for the gap between the barrier and the truck. Just a mere brush with death it was. The bike and Slim just slipped through to the tune of British labor screaming bloody fool.

Before long and still alive, Slim and cycle were riding the ferry from Hamlet's castle on the Danish island across to Sweden. It's a short distance and a quick trip so Slim had maneuvered the bike to the very front and waited so that when the ramp slammed down onto the quay, he had the motor rumbling and was off. He hit Sweden running and was funneled right into downtown where the traffic didn't take too kindly to his appearance. They all stood on their horns at once and were coming right at him. Bloody hell and God bless the ignorant! Unbeknownst to Slim, the Swedes were sticking with the English and still driving on the left hand side of the road. Go left young man, go left! It was a heart beater but Slim and Triumph escaped with only a case of embarrassment.

Back in the USA, his friend and the bike had returned unscathed. The Triumph was still brand new and pristine and looking for trouble. Slim had it out one day on some mission taking him through the affluent, leafy suburbs. It was a drizzly day in autumn and the street was plastered with blown leaves when an oblivious housewife on an errand to the grocery store pulled out of a side street right in front of him. The brakes on that cycle, both front wheel and back, were on the handlebars and Slim jammed them hard. The bike went down in a flash, hit the asphalt sideways and skidded across the leafy wet to a stop in the middle of the intersection with Slim, outraged, watching the woman forever oblivious, motoring away. Once again both man and machine suffered little to no damage but the message was clear – you never knew where the next challenge to life, limb and motorcycle was to come from.

Slim and his buddy, co-owners of this magnificent machine, at the time were indentured to a large northeastern university and one of the perks provided by the same was a chain link pen especially for bicycles and motorcycles. Instead of leaving the Triumph chained to a tree or a fire hydrant, they would park it comfortably in the pen chained and padlocked to the fence. It was clearly the resident star of that particular enclosure – a prince among foundlings – and was visible, advertising its star power, from the street. The street and the cycle pen were sandwiched between and among college dormitories but that didn't stop two guys from slipping in late one night carrying long handled bolt cutters.

There was at that time and I imagine there still is, a severe town vs. gown dichotomy. The university was situated smack in the middle of town and held much of the most desirable real estate. The town, or city as it were, also was home to extensive working class neighborhoods which yielded a population of 'tough' kids who harbored no love for the stuck-up intellectual snobs of the university. This situation led to occasional circumstances and it also led to the university employing its own private police force. This force numbered quite a few cops. They were divided into day and night shifts and they carried guns. Nobody could remember when a university cop had actually used his gun but there they were and nobody thought twice about it.

One of these rent-a-cops, making his rounds on the night shift, walking the street between the dorm buildings, noticed something going on in the cycle pen. He crouched against the brick wall of an adjacent dormitory and watched to make sure of what he was seeing. Suddenly a motorcycle engine boomed into life and the Triumph ripped through the gate with two guys on it, hit the street and turned in his direction. He stepped into the street and held his hands out to block their passage. No way in hell thought the driver and he punched the accelerator – we already know what happens to that Triumph when you do that – and bore down on that cop like a beast possessed. He jumped and rolled as the cycle blasted by, came up trying to unbutton the restraining strap, pulled out the pistol and fired three shots at the fast retreating cycle.

The next morning the university was abuzz. A privately employed university security guard had actually shot somebody. Who was this cop? What training did he have? Who is in charge of this security force? Why are they allowed to carry loaded pistols? Who authorized the use of guns anyway? Is it moral to shoot someone because he is a thief? It was as if no one quite realized that these rent-a-cops roamed the campus with loaded pistols and the affair engendered a university wide soul searching.

Slim, however, did not have to search his own soul. He was well aware that he had already sold his in exchange for ownership of that machine. The machine that had killed Lawrence. The machine that promised very expensive thrills. The machine that was sleek and shiny, that gave you speed and power and unlimited freedom and a promise of engineered bliss. You could have everything promised but only in exchange for making a pact. A pact that included the understanding that one day would come a reckoning – a reckoning that might steal your soul but more likely would require a pound of flesh and a beaker of blood.

The Triumph disappeared around the corner under the streetlights and disappeared from Slim's life. It was never seen or heard of again but the boy who was riding on the back as his buddy was accelerating away was dropped off at the hospital ten minutes later with two bullets in his back. The city detective who spoke to Slim said the kid refused to divulge the name of his partner and would be forced to pay back the value of the bike and the case was closed.

The motorcycle that always looked for trouble had found it and its day of reckoning had arrived, extracting flesh and blood, and one poor kid who was out on a lark – hey, let's steal that Bonneville – paid the Devil.

THE BOY SCOUT

Old Slimshanks was walking alone through the night along an avenue in Rotterdam headed back to his rental room when he was accosted by a drunk. He was in the Netherlands for the summer having gotten a temporary job in an oil refinery a few miles outside of the city. The refinery was ensconced behind two dikes – one a wall edging the North Atlantic and the other defining a canal so close that the transiting tankers loomed incongruously high above the men working below sea level. Slim was there as a result of a special arrangement and had no experience as a rough-neck or any desire to become one so the foreman had to make work or even invent jobs to keep him busy. Basically all the Dutch had been educated from early childhood to speak English. See that pile of rebar over there? Clean it up and stack it over here. Take this cutting torch. You know how to use a cutting torch? Cut up, how do you say in English, these metals into pieces this long. OK?

The guys on the job all belonged to a union and the union insisted on smoke breaks every two hours. They loved their tobacco more than they loved their lunch and the company erected fireproof concrete bunkers where they all collected to roll and smoke. They rolled their own cigarettes from pouches of 'shag'. The 250 milligram packets of shag tobacco could be purchased anywhere in Holland and they came under various brand names and three grades – svar, half-svar (haulef), and light (likt). Each of the men had his favorite and there were endless debates as to the merits and lack thereof of each, and, since Slim was a new free agent he was subject to proselytizing and recommendations on shape, size, rolling techniques and even correct licking procedures. Even though Slim was not a smoker he felt obliged to join the club and when he finally made his choice of brand and color, Samson half-svar, he was met with a chorus of cheers, boos and catcalls.

He rented a room that summer right in the city in a house owned by a sweet little old lady who spoke no English but carried on long conversations with him over tea kept warm in a flowery cozy and served in delicate china cups that might have belonged to Queen Victoria. She had lived through the Second World War and he could see the horror and grief in her face as she described the terrible bombing that destroyed Rotterdam. Slim said what about these tea cups and she teared up indicating that they survived when many things and people did not. Even though they shared no common language, she liked his company and told him long and, he supposed, intricate stories about, he supposed, curious and heart-breaking happenings in her youth. He had a separate key to the front door and his room was at the back of the ground floor so that he could come in at any hour and not disturb her, although occasionally she would be sitting up in the kitchen and tut, tut him like his mother for coming home so late.

It wasn't so late, as Slim strolled through the city back to her house, the night this drunk staggered up to him and started yammering. Inches from his face, the drunk was blowing fumes and spittle and yammering a mile-a-minute incomprehensibly in Dutch. Slim tried to move back out of his orbit, threw up his hands and said, in English of course, how he had no idea what you're talking about. This seemed to aggravate the man somewhat and he just upped the volume and began vociferating more energetically, waving his arms and turning red in the face. Slim backed up some more and kept talking: I'm sure you're right. Whatever you say. Everything's cool buddy boy. You're drunk as a skunk. Wouldn't this be a good time to head home? The more Slim talked, the more furious the man became until he sputtered out – no English, you Nederlander man. Was that what was bothering him? He thought Slim was a Dutchman who was just fooling with him. No, no said Slim, I'm an American. No America you. You bullshit. With that Slim started to laugh and the drunken fool, who was dressed in a jacket and a tie that was pulled down from his collar, struggled mightily out of his jacket, tossed it on the ground between them and began doing a St.Vitus dance and brandishing his fists. Put up your dukes!

Now to set the scene properly let's describe the two men. Slim was 6'3", pretty strong, had been an athlete and was still in very good shape. The furious and very drunk Dutchman was probably 5'9", dumpy, and was tripping over his own feet. So Slim thought this was all a nuisance and a joke and for some reason unknown, after the jacket hit the pavement in front of him, Slim worked his right foot under it, lifted it in the air and kicked out. As if in slow motion, Slim watched the jacket miraculously open and spread like a parachute and settle down right on top of and over the poor guy still doing his St.Vitus dance. Slim stood and watched in amazement as the man began thrashing and flailing and yowling as if an Andean condor had dropped out of the sky onto him. It was as if he were fighting his way out of a paper bag and not succeeding and it struck Slim as so funny he began squeezing out tears of laughter. The man dervished all over the sidewalk, spinning and punching his way out from under that jacket and Slim was incredulous with laughter until the damn fool windmilled out into the open and smashed a fist right into Slim's face. Into his nose, and blood sprayed everywhere and he knew right away that it was broken.

Now Slim wasn't a fighter. He didn't want to fight anybody. He had never been in a fist fight in his life. It usually wasn't necessary. His size and his demeanor seemed to dampen the enthusiasm of any possible aggressor. But he was confident he could defend himself if he had to and he certainly wasn't any holy man, so when this idiot came windmilling out of nowhere and busted his nose he was at first paralyzed and unbelieving – did this really just happen? – and then consumed with a blinding, red rage. He went after that guy with all the hatred and vengeance that arises out of the most primitive heart of men and tore into him until he was saved, that is, Slim was saved, by a God-sent intervention. They were three young toughs, street thugs, who saw the action, skidded their car to the curb, jumped out and ran to join the fray. The red veil lifted from Slim's eyes and he said: He's a stupid drunk. I'm just defending myself. You an American? Yes. OK, and they turned from Slim to pounce on the man with no jacket, shirtfront red with Slim's blood. Slim walked away and didn't look back.

Well, bloody hell, to quote the unknown Englishman, Slim pondered as he walked away. Who was the damn fool in this one? He, trapped in his own jacket flailing like a blind man being led to the gallows or you, standing there careless and laughing as if you were on a pedestal, untouchable? Blind, drunken stupidity wins over hubris? Walk away from trouble has always been your mantra. That might or might not have worked this time. But the guy was so innocuous. Would a boy scout have been prepared? Bloody hell.

I hope she is not awake and sitting up for me. What a fuss she would make. She will mother me to pieces. Maybe I can slip in quiet.

She was sitting there as he came stealthily through the door. She clucked her tongue and shook her head a few times and said, he thought, I have seen whole streets running with blood. This is nothing. Splash some water on your face and go to bed.

{ 3 }

SURVIVOR

As an unmarried enlisted man in the U.S. Army occupying the Panama Canal Zone in the 1970's you were expected to live in the barracks. In high-ceilinged, open screened, stuccoed buildings, the iron-framed beds were set up in rows 4ft apart with a hinged trunk at the foot of each. The beds had to be made just so every morning and all the G.I.'s worldly possessions were kept in that trunk. There were periodic inspections during which a staff sergeant would walk through checking the beds, the shine on the boots and the condition of the trunks. The trunks contained a top tray that pulled up and out and the army issued each soldier a diagram that indicated exactly where and how oriented each item of personal care would be placed in that tray. The toothbrush must be pristine and placed in its designated spot with the bristles facing left next to the toothpaste pointing up. The razor must be a safety razor and again positioned just so. Every item on the diagram must be included in your array even if you never intend to use them. One item that Slim found silly and somewhat humorous was deodorant. Deodorant. Imagine men who have been trained to slice up other men with bayonets and spend months festering in fox holes being forced to buy deodorant. It was so silly that Old Slimshanks devised the what-me-worry stratagem of outfitting the upper tray with brand new stuff in their specified locations on a newly washed sheet and never touching them again.

This strategy really proved its merit once Slim realized that the only evening entertainment for the boys in the barracks was smoking weed and listening to the frogs. To give them their due, the frogs did put on quite a show. These were tropical rainforest frogs who had found a second home in the storm drains of the army base. The boys would smoke it up and then sit down on the curb next to the sewer grating and take in the show. Those frogs didn't just croak or trill as did your average frog back home; they were melodic; they sang; they crooned. One night several years later just recently returned home and riding with a friend through the canyons of New York City, Slim was boggled when he pushed the radio button and out poured the very same singing of the very same rain forest frogs. Boggled by the coincidence and the memories and wondering if the nature recorder hadn't stuck his microphone down the very same army base sewer grating. Howsoever it was with the frogs, at the time the long term value of this entertainment looked to be pretty low so Slim made up his bed tight and crisp, left all the untouched trunk items in order and moved out of the base into Panama.

The army became like a job to which he commuted every day with week-ends usually free. But it was often tedious and repetitive work featuring a lot of papers in triplicate. After all, even though this was during the Vietnam era, there was no war to fight in Panama and no urgencies other than keeping the trucks washed and running. In the Canal Zone throughout the 20th century the U.S. military had created a massive infrastructure. Besides barracks and offices and family housing with lawns and gardens, there were theaters and gymnasia and hospitals and airfields and motor pools and PXs and beaches and tennis courts and swimming pools. There were also an airborne training facility on one of the bases, the School of the Americas on another and an ongoing jungle survival course. As part of a crusade to alleviate the daily tedium, Slim was willing to volunteer for any or all of these offerings. However, he was introduced to the School of the Americas the day he arrived in Panama.

Upon entering the army, your in-service career would be mapped out without your knowledge before you had even finished basic training. The army had it figured for Slim that he would be taught to speak Spanish, trained to repair 'small' weapons and then teach the repair at the School of the Americas. The Spanish course was intensive conversational for six months with a Cuban refugee for a teacher. The small weapons repair was two months of dismantling and remantling all GI issue firearms between a 45 pistol and a 50 caliber machine gun. The School of the Americas Slim had no idea about. He didn't know he was to go there or even that it existed. Due to an incredible slice of good fortune, he was met on the tarmac as he dismounted the military C-130 in the Canal Zone not only by a blast of super-heated air and tropical humidity but also by a college classmate whom he didn't know but who had recognized his name on the dossier of incomings for that day. He asked to see Slim's orders and said, "That's the School of the Americas! You're not going there." What do you mean? Those are my orders. Don't I have to report there? "Trust me, you do not want to be involved with the School of the Americas. We'll find someplace else for you."

This was a revelation to Slim, that a lot of power and control in the military rests with the clerks and many of the clerks in the army at that time were college graduates the same age as Slim who were drafted or enlisted, didn't want to be officers and were designated to be clerks because they could read, write and think. Most of them did not appreciate being in the army, didn't want to have anything to do with the Vietnam fiasco, and had formed a sort of sub-rosa brotherhood operating under the generals' radar. So Slim's savior, who had been chosen as an aide to one of the Canal Zone's generals, explained that it was only a matter of making a few phone calls to fellow brothers in personnel and his orders would be buried, new ones typed up, and he would be reassigned to a unit more to his liking. Well, Hallelujah! But what's up with the School of the Americas? Plenty. They are bringing in military from all over Latin America, training them in tactics to beat down 'communist' insurgencies and sending them home with a boatload of weapons. Now I see what my orders would have me doing. Sure. You definitely don't want to be stuck in that situation. They are also operating a scam under the cover of the USAID program. They are cleaning out the store of antique military junk they don't want any more like M-14 rifles left over from WWII, and giving the stuff to these Latin America dictators, writing it in the books at market value and adding it in to pad the total figure of AID given out to supposedly help the underdeveloped Latin countries.

The School of the Americas later became notorious for training the guys who brought down Che in Bolivia and Slim was more than happy to have had nothing to do with it. His tarmac savior wrangled an assignment to a Civil Affairs unit which featured doctors, veterinarians and engineers who were involved with problems or crises among the local civilian population. The whole unit was also certified airborne so Slim was more than happy to escape the day-to-day for two weeks and attend jump school. Airborne training of course featured jumping out of airplanes but more than that it involved doing a lot of pushups, maintaining skinned sidewalls for a haircut and spit-shining your boots. If you were less than enthusiastic about either or both of these latter items you were singled out for severe harassment. The sergeants running the show presumably didn't care about your deodorant problems but they had a fixation for shiny boots. By the end of a day's workout your boots would be soaked, lacerated and plastered with mud but they had to be spit-shined every morning for inspection. The reasoning behind continually reshining a boot which was doomed to instantly revert to its native condition, was something Slim could not fathom but when you're in thrall to the powers that be, and they dictate a spit-shine, then that's what you do. However, fully aware he wasn't up to the challenge, Slim made a deal with the Kuna man who cleaned the barracks. He offered him whatever he wanted in exchange for taking care of Slim's boots every night and having them shined for the following morning. Slim figured this kind of miracle was beyond even Jesus Christ but that Kuna came into the barracks smiling every morning at daybreak and presented Slim with dry and shiny boots.

The airborne troopers who ran the school considered themselves members of an exclusive club of the toughest hombres on the planet and weren't too happy about allowing Slim to join but seeing that he could do pushups forever, kept his sidewalls skinned and had the shiniest boots on the ground, they had no choice but to hand over a diploma. By the time his hair had grown out and his boots were back to normal, Slim was ready for another diversion and the jungle survival course promised to be entertaining.

The jungle survival program had been set up in the Canal Zone apparently in response to the fracas in Vietnam in order to give the boys headed that way a taste of what they were getting into. They were running groups of ten to fifteen through there all the time and to get into it all you had to do was volunteer. The course was only to be a two day and one night affair and the only supplies the group was allowed were one machete and the clothes on their backs. They were also each given a special hat – a soft-bodied, floppy brimmed, olive drab hat which you had to hold in hand so as not to lose it as you jumped out of a helicopter into the river to start out. The hat had great significance. You were informed before beginning that there would be 'hostiles' in the jungle somewhere along the path and they would be trying to take your hat. If you lost your hat to a hostile, that would be tantamount to losing your head under actual conditions of war.

They were a group of ten ranked by an army colonel. They hauled out dripping, made sure of their hats and walked off single file along a well-trod path. Slim was the lowest ranking member so he was given the machete to carry. Their instructions were to walk the path, bivouac the night somewhere and, somehow, come out on the other end whenever they got there – it would be apparent – and watch out for the wicked hostiles. But this was really a walk in the woods thought Slim as they squished in their boots along a way open through the bush that had obviously been tramped many times before. There appeared an occasional monkey and there were some bird sounds to be heard but otherwise it was a hot, damp, green blur moving by them at the speed of a walk. Nothing going on muttered Slim as he trudged along, but ahead, at the front of the line there was some commotion. Could be hostiles he thought but the line kept moving and as he got closer, he saw a Choco male bare to the waist with parrot feathers in a headband standing beside the trail looking actually quite benevolent As each soldier passed, he uttered possibly the only English he knew "hat please" and each guy happily flipped off his hat and handed it over. Slim, at the end of the line, shrugged and did the same. When he looked back, the Indian with his pile of hats had already disappeared. "What the hell was that all about?" Slim asked the man in front of him. Well, the Choco gets a dollar for every hat he turns in to HQ and we're happy to help him out. Those tricky, wily, bloodthirsty hostiles turned out to be friendly Indians in league hat in hand with friendly American soldiers. Was I the only one who didn't know about this? thought Slim as they moved on through the gathering gloom of the oncoming evening and emerged into a small clearing showing the remnants of a shelter in the center.

Let's stay here for the night. Some other group put this together out of branches and sticks. The roof needs fixing. If we can collect enough leaves or branches or stuff to make a cover, maybe we can sleep out of the rain tonight. There happened to be some sort of palm, the only tree left in the clearing, growing off to one side of the shanty. Hey! Look at this palm tree. If we cut it down, we could use the branches to thatch the roof. Yeah, yeah, good idea. Give me that machete. It was a good sized tree – 20–25' high and 10-12" thick. Probably the reason it was the only tree left in the clearing. They took turns whacking at the trunk and as the notch widened and deepened, Slim looked up at the crown and studied the tree for a moment. In a non-committal tone he said, "Which way do you think it's going to fall?" The action suddenly stopped for a brief interval before the colonel jumped in pulling rank and said: Private Slim is always a wise ass. Get on with the job boys. Just in case, he said, you, you, and you push on this side of the tree. They went back to chopping and, as the last fibers holding the trunk stretched and squealed, the tree started to go. The three guys designated as counter pushers began to yell: It's coming this way! Holy shit! It's heavy! We can't hold it! Others scrambled in beside them to help but, as if it were all predetermined and inevitable, impelled by its own gravitas, the palm knocked them over as if they were so many bowling pins and crashed squarely through the middle of their nighttime home.

In the tropical rainforest, the temperature typically hovers in the 90s. That is, except during the night when it seems to plunge precipitously. That plunge in the tropics however, might take the thermometer only to 70. But when you are sleeping out in the open on the ground in the rain without any blanket, 70 puts you into quite a shiver. So they were a low-caloried and somewhat dispirited bunch when they emerged the following day at the end of the trail into the dazzling light of a parking lot. There was an army truck waiting for them, and on the road back to a hot shower Slim contemplated the hard-won lessons learned by way of this survival course. In order to survive in the jungle, you must, first, not argue with any hostile – give him whatever he wants – and, second, when you're waist deep in the big muddy and the big fool says to keep on, just follow orders, cross your fingers and hope to make it out of the morass.

THE GIRL WHO LOVED THE LITTLE PIGGY

Old Slimshanks once owned a vehicle which he named the little piggy – 'El Cochinito' in Spanish, which fit the circumstances because this was in Panama, in the Canal Zone, and out. It was a '63 VW beetle which he had gotten off a fellow conscript in the US army whose term was finished so he was going home and leaving his beetle behind. It had seen better days, as they say, to the extent that a bungee cord was needed to keep it from popping out of 4th gear, and the floor under the driver's seat had disintegrated to the point where a square of plywood covered the hole and the seat sat unmoored on top of it. It was often with mildly sadistic pleasure that Slim would watch someone borrow the car for the first time and teeter over backwards upon engaging 1st gear. It was only running fueled by memory and nostalgia but Slim liked it for tooling around the narrow twisting streets of Old Panama.

Old Panama is the part of the city built by the Spaniards

starting in the 1500's on a promontory reaching into the Pacific and forgotten by the gleaming white towers of hotels, condos, apartments and casinos erected uptown along the strand. He liked the Cochinito because if he left it never locked in the old town nobody would be likely to steal it, and since the Panamanian drivers were always bouncing their cars off of each other, the more they crunched it, the more he liked it. He even laughed when they eased a large truck into his rear end while he was waiting for a light to change. He scrambled out and onto the truck's running board, put his face in the window and commenced to call the truck man every curse he had ever learned in Spanish. But he didn't know enough to match the effortless and lengthy cursing of the average Panamanian. He just stacked the words one on top of the other until the driver cracked up at this gringo pouring out a demented stream of local stupidities. It would be like reeling off in someone's face – asshole, shithead, dumb fuck, knucklehead, mutton brain, son of the fattest whore in the world, trip over your own testicles dude, troglodyte, sputter, sputter. He laughed and said Gringo, don't get excited. I read what it says there and this won't make any difference to the taste of the meat.

He was referring to a quote which Slim had had hand painted across the back under the rear window. It said, "El pelo de la res no influye en el sabor de la carne." Slim had lifted it out of an Argentine story he had recently read. It's a take on not judging a book by its cover – but this is beef by the hair of its skin. It was done fancy in multi colors by a professional 'chiva' bus painter, of which there are plenty in Panama. These chivas (buses) were ubiquitous in Panama. It seemed like anybody could get in on the act starting with the bare bones of a truck. Start with a frame and build your own emporium on wheels good for carrying four people or an entire village depending on your degree of megalomania But what really sets them apart is the degree of decoration. They could be festooned with multicolored fringes, bangled with chromed widgets, bejeweled with a thousand lights and painted the gaudier the better. And they all had names painted on as careful as embroidery like 'El Tigre' or 'El Amigo de Dios' or 'El Rey del Camino'.

So many chivas honking the streets full in Panama City and plenty of painters to decorate them so Slim commissioned one to apply the quote beautifully to the sloping backside of the Cochinito. He was prompted to do this by a midnight raid on the old beetle. Some 'friends' decided that a new paint job was called for and did it themselves out of whatever cans they had on hand so Slim figured to finish the job with a touch of professionalism. The car attracted attention – that is, you couldn't miss it, so things happened – like late one night a Canal Zone cop came up close behind and after a bit turned on his light, walked up and leaned in on Slim grinning, apparently for the sole purpose of saying "Does that mean that a blonde will taste the same as a redhead?"

The trucker who rammed him did it on purpose, not because of the "pelo de la res" but because the Cochinito carried a Canal Zone license plate. This shitcan of a VW belonged to a gringo, that plate said, and the gringos (that is, the

Americans) were being less and less appreciated at that time in Panama. There were signs all over the city posted by the reigning general which said: "On our feet or dead but never on our knees." This was General Omar Torrijos who had taken power in a coup and was applying heat to the Americans to give up the Canal Zone. He was ratcheting up the rhetoric and the pressure while simultaneously buttoning down the Panamanian street life. There were police everywhere and these weren't just ordinary cops but specially chosen or recruited army personnel called 'El Guardia'. They carried batons and guns and were characterized by berets, tight form-fitting uniforms which displayed pretty much universally muscular bodies.

You didn't mess with the Guardia. They must have smiled and laughed like everyday humans at some point in their lives but any semblance of a sense of humor seemed to have been trained right out of them, so it was unfortunate one day when Slim lost his bearings somewhat in the rabbit warren of the old city and careened the Cochinito on two wheels around the corner to find himself and his girlfriend right in front of the Presidential Palace. The place is called 'El Palacio de las Garzas' (The Palace of the Herons) because at some point in its history the herons had free range of its fountain and courtyard. It is a piece of colonial splendor situated close by the ocean and it was being patrolled by a bevy of Guardia. These Guardia had exchanged their holstered pistols for what looked like WW1 carbines with bayonets fixed and the abrupt arrival of the mighty little piggy skidding and fishtailing toward them caused them to lower bayonets and charge. I give up! cried Slim and it didn't take them but an instant to haul him out, crow hop him to the nearest wall, spread eagle his arms and hands against the wall and rifle butt his ankles to a straddle.

These guys had been so bored for so long on this Presidential Palace detail where nothing ever happened except arrivals and departures of limousines, that they were overcome with joy at the opportunity to wrestle down and capture an obviously berserk bomber. Slim just started talking and talking and kept talking, telling them anything and everything he could conjure up to cool their ardor. He said he was an important guy in the US Army. That his unit was a Civil Affairs group. That they worked together often with the Panamanian government and the Guardia, but, as he was trying to remember the name of the Guardia colonel who he had met once at the base, the chief of the Guardia ordered two of his thugs to search the car. At that moment Slim's Panamanian girlfriend stepped out of the beetle holding a bag in one hand like a purse and walked to the group around Slim. The Guardia curiously stood silent while she, just as cool and natural and poised as if she had been practicing this routine forever, said, "Roberto, I have some things to take care of at home. I'm sure everything will be fine here. I'll see you tomorrow." And she turned and with some insouciance walked away shifting the bag as if it were a purse to cradle it in the crook of an elbow.

The spell broken, they searched the Cochinito and found nothing to incriminate him as a terrorist bent on exploding the Presidential Palace. Meanwhile the colonel's name popped into his head which Slim kept repeating as if it were a magic charm and insisting on calling him to verify their professional relationship, which of course was non-existent. The Palace Guardia started to mutter in tones of disappointment as they sensed their prey slipping away. He knows Colonel Rodriguez. He must be important. Then why is he driving this shitty little fuck-up of a car? Slim jumped in and directed their attention to the 'dicho' painted on the back and said see this message? It says you can't judge the man by the car he drives. One of them actually chuckled which drew a dirty look from the chief who turned to Slim and told him to get the hell out of here with that shitball carrito 'carrito de mierda' and now that you know where is the Palace don't ever try this again.

No chance of that mused Slim as he drove thoughtfully back uptown. That was shaky. That actually was way too close. If it weren't for that girl. What smarts. What brass. Quick thinking. She saved my bacon. You never know until the game is on the line what a person's got. She had been Slim's lover for about a year and they had spent plenty of time together. They had even driven far up-country a few times to dive into the dance halls that were lit up every Saturday night. The volume was high, the rhythms full speed and she hung on to him until he was able to stay abreast of the swirling tides. She was tall, slim, coffee colored, sassy and acted like she owned this city, this country, even though her family was perhaps lower middle class living in a barrio on the outer edge of the city. She had wit and sparkle and a mouth that could back talk with anyone but Slim never would have imagined her sizing up this situation, collecting that bag from the back seat which he was transporting for a friend, sauntering in no rush through a gaggle of Guardia to say goodbye, and walking away with ½ pound of marijuana under her arm.

{ 5 }

NOT JUST A DANCE

In those days in Panama when General Torrijos had the country locked down with his Guardia Nacional, he didn't just believe in the stick but also wielded the carrot. Outside of Panama City, Colón, and a few other small towns, the isthmus was a campesino's country. Rice and beans, bullocks and wagons, homemade leather sandals and particularly patterned straw hats, it was a matter of wresting a daily living out of the red earth and the tropical weather. The daily grind was tortuous using animal power and hand tools, and what was there to look forward to? Well, securing the harvest was satisfying and anticipating your children was also, but really, Saturday night and the upcoming dance was what motivated the average campesino through his work week. The General knew this and, in the spirit of 'let them eat cake', promoted this dance and this 'musica tipica' throughout the country. If the country people could get roaring drunk and have a rousing good blow-out once a week, that might keep their minds off the fact that he had them locked in straight-jackets. However, they didn't consider this, they just loved their dance.

Old Slimshanks had never given any of this a second thought until the girl-who-loved-the-little-piggy suggested they take the Cochinito and ride the road upcountry to one of these dances. That road is the Pan-American Highway, the only road through Panama from the Costa Rican border to the Canal. At this time in the early 70s the Americans had recently financed and engineered and straightened and banked and concreted the highway such that Slim, who by sheer happenstance was once driving the Alpha Romeo of an acquaintance who was feeling queasy, looked at the speedometer to notice with curiosity that he was going 125 miles per hour. Miles of open road and nobody and nothing in sight except for an occasional military transport allowed the Cochinito to snuffle along at 40 or 50 to arrive at one of the towns or villages famous throughout the country for their dance bands. These towns, one of which is Ocú (OhCoo), are all located on branch roads sometimes far off the highway and had built enclosed and covered pavilions especially to host the dance. On first seeing one, Slim was amazed at the sheer size of it. As wide as and half the length of a football field, these venues were built to accommodate large numbers of people.

In the evening in Panama City when the sea breeze was starting to come in and the days heat beginning to seep away, Slim would venture out onto the balcony and almost every night he could hear what he realized, after some time, was music. Not obvious, it sounded like this: "ding dida, ding dida, dingdingding." It was coming from downtown he knew not where. It was faint, far away and in the air almost every night. Slim wondered for a long time what was it all about. Finally the girl, who cocked her head, squinted at him and questioned how anybody could be so clueless, informed him it was dance music coming from the big dance hall in the city. She said it was 'musica tipica', real Panamanian country music loved by the campesinos and disparaged by the upper class who referred to the music as 'PingDing'. There were plenty of country folk come to the big city looking for work. Paying jobs. Menial labor for the unskilled. Street sweeping for the men, and maids, au pairs and prostitution for the young women. Any night they could collect at the dance hall, come together, pair off and dance to the pingding. Slim never did hunt down the dance hall to check out the city version of the dance so when the girl suggested they hop in the Cochinito and head to Ocú, he had no idea what he was in for.

The music varied somewhat according to which conjunto was playing and each band stuck to its home town or to its chosen town as it were. So if you were going to Ocú you already knew who would be playing. The bands were known and named after their leaders who invariably played accordion. Behind the accordion was invariably a stoical dude on the conga drums along with a bass player and some guitar. Each piece had a title and lyrics and they all sang along to the microphones in front of them. The musical style, if it had to be classified, was a version of cumbia. Cumbia is associated with Colombia but that's not surprising because before Teddy Roosevelt happened along with his big stick and his plans for a canal, Panama and Colombia were one country.

The conjunto was bound by, I always assumed, a social con-tract with its public to put out the music 'hasta amanacer', until dawn. Until dawn, now we're getting into it. Starting just after the sun sets in the evening, which in the tropics would be around 9.00 o'clock and putting it out until maybe 5.00 in the morning. This is not your average evening soiree. This is a serious enterprise. Let's see how it goes.

The evening commenced with the grandmothers dancing with their grandsons and grandfathers with their grand-daughters along with associated great uncles and aunts and children slowly gravitating around the oval floor always counter clockwise. Meanwhile, as the night crept in, prime time candidates began to trickle in from the surrounding countryside, nearby villages, and some adventurous souls from the big city. Campesinos and cowboys and young studs and older girls and younger women all coming in like moths around the candle. Many of the men carried bottles of rum. That would be rum classified as 'white lightning'- clear as water transported in a bottle long bereft of any label and stoppered with a corn cob. The women chattered and laughed and gathered in groups around the periphery. Slowly the old folks and children began to drop out and dis-appear and things began to heat up. Some of the older men would stay around to pluck a woman from off the edge and put on a virtuoso display of elegant dancing, going coun-terflow twirling around the edges backwards and forwards always with the music but staying a couple of inches away from her.

Along about midnight those inches diminished to negative numbers. Now the incoming tide had reached flood stage and the dance floor was full of bodies plastered up against each other. The scene would be recognizable to anyone who has participated in a country dance in Texas. Doing the two-step there, they would all be going around in one direction at top speed, the men driving forward as if piloting a semi, and the women floating along incredibly going backwards. However in Ocú, we are dancing through the tropical night in an open arena following the accordion as he rollicks the keys up and down and all around that cumbia. It gets sweaty and it gets steamy and about as sexed up as any group of humans could be.

One of the more famous dance band leaders at the time had acquired a nickname. It went like this – 'El poste de macaro negro'. The 'poste' could be considered to be a post or a trunk and 'macaro negro' was and is a local tree which yielded a wood remarkable for its hardness. You get the message, and it was said that every off season produced a slew of babies fathered by the same 'poste'. (The dance took place mainly during the dry season, December through May). This phenomenon might be explained various ways. One could come under the rubric of 'it takes a village to raise a child'. That is to say a young woman's mind-set around sex and babies was more expansive in the setting of old style country and village life. You weren't disparaged or exiled for having a baby without an immediate father; the collective village just shrugged and took care of you and the baby, especially if the sperm donor was known to be the famous 'poste'. Another explanation is the obvious one that these dances were the time for sexual liaisons to form and as we know, sex happens – it's a bumper sticker. Old Slim watched as yet another couple would slowly disappear into the darkness outside and he wasn't immune to the fervor. He listened to the accordion romping along doubletime and, attached like a limpet to the girl who loved the little piggy, he romped along with the crowd while she taught him with her body to really get it and grow to love that crazy dance.

The first time Slim went to the dance in Ocú, while the affair was in full swing, he thought he was hearing dogs or wolves or coyotes or owls outside beyond the light of the arena howling or yelping or hooting. It was a wild, somewhat unearthly sound and she took him out there to see. What was to see was a group of older peasants wearing their little pork-pie straw hats and their leather sandals collected into a circle, each with his arms across the shoulders of the next until they were bound into a tight round with their heads all facing inwards like the spokes of a wheel. And they were hooting in unison. The sound produced was unclassifiable but if you were to combine yodeling with throat singing with an old rubber bulb automotive claxon, you might approximate what they were sending out into the Panamanian night. It was a repetitive and ongoing ooah, ooah which, Slim realized after begging into a circle one night, was a mind blower. First of all, you quickly began to hyperventilate and then the collective sounds commenced to hang on to each other, dissolve, recombine and resonate and reverberate inside your skull. 'Twas like going for a ride to never-never land on a tuning fork. So there it was: You came out of it stoned. Combine that with white lightning in a bottle, the music barreling along with the intensity of an interstate loaded with semis, the heat, the sweat and the promise of sex somewhere, and it's well after midnight heading into the witching hours.

These villages stuck out in the countryside throughout Latin America are almost always built along the same lines. There are no white picket fences enclosing little mown lawns and flower gardens differentiating individual houses. There are often also no sidewalks from which you may look into those lawns, gardens and front porches. The villages are modeled on the Spanish towns from which came the conquistadores. The habitations look inward to a courtyard not out to the street. The pedestrian is presented with nothing so much as tall adobe walls on both sides punctuated by large doorways leading into the courtyards. The courtyards are often pleasing spaces featuring any assortment of greenery, water and flowers. However, as a stranger, you are very unlikely to ever see these unless you are lucky enough to be directly invited. So it was that in Ocú or Las Tablas or any other Panamanian dance hall town where there were no street lights during the witching hours in the steamy dark, Old Slimshanks and his lover, revved up to the point of no return, found themselves up against an adobe wall, she, with her dress up around her waist, pinned like a butterfly into a display case.

So in these circumstances, what do you do for an encore? Well, you go back to the dance of course. Jump back into the maelstrom until you don't know backwards from forwards and who knows, you might blindly grope your way back to another adobe wall, and the beat goes on until the music stops and the sun rises to reveal tattered and battered humans, some comatose, others exhausted and hollow-eyed but strangely exhilarated and triumphant ready to take on the toils of yet another week.

{ 6 }

HITCH HIKE

Fraught. That's a word for you. Fraught with danger. Fraught with possibilities. Fraught with unknowns. When you stay in your home town always bumping into people you know things are less fraught than if you are walking an unknown trail in an unknown jungle and you are about to encounter unknown human beings. Unknown human beings are always fraught with possibility. A yellow flag waves somewhere deep flickering ever so slightly behind your eyes whenever you deal with one. Families, tribes, brotherhoods, secret societies hold you in situations less fraught and protect you from fear of the unknown man. For millennia, somebody caught beyond the boundaries and without the fellowship of the group would likely be in trouble. But so as not to get too over fraught here, lets move to the question in play which is: How fraught are things when you open the door on an unknown driver of car or truck, slide into the close confines next to him and wheel on down the road to wherever his whim might take you? The answer is – plenty fraught. Things happen when you hitchhike. Almost by definition things are going to happen, good, bad or ugly. Every time someone else stops to pick you up, the yellow flags are flickering, almost invisibly, but there, and the possibilities are fraught.

Old Slimshanks did plenty of hitchhiking in his day and things did happen to him, mostly good, some bad and none ugly. Some guys would give him a ride, lonely men in pick-ups, who would just want to talk and they'd drop him off twenty five miles down the road before cutting off onto dirt byways. Others were quiet long distance drivers who wanted Slim to talk his life and tell his stories. Hardly ever a woman stopped for him and he understood why and didn't blame them Those who did, he admired their courage and wondered what they were thinking but didn't probe so as not to scare them. Although yellow flags always flew, Slim was gratified at how friendly and undemanding most everybody was, and many rides led to places he would have missed and to situations out of mind.

One driver left him in Gallup, New Mexico at 2 a.m., yanking his door open against which he had been drowsing, telling him to get out, that he was dead weight. This guy had picked up Slim in central Texas saying he was headed to L.A. and was looking for some company. He was broadcasting sweetness and light and full of hippie talk common enough during those years of the early seventies, so even though Slim had been planning to visit friends at the Navajo reservation, he decided to stay with this one ride all the way to the California coast. But dead weight he had become, and as the guy peeled off into the night leaving Slim under the orange sodium glare of a gas station/bus depot, Slim mused that he must have embittered some during those long lonely night-time hours – must have obsessed on what poor company Slim was sleeping against the door. But, look on the bright side, he thought as he trudged out of the sodium glare into the fluorescence of the bus depot. Here he was on the very edge of the Navajo reservation, it's only a few hours till dawn and maybe he could catch up on his friends after all.

He was the only soul in the depot, sitting in the cold blue light and snoozing in the middle of a row of red plastic seats when a bus pulled in, dropped off a few people and left in a blast of diesel. The few dissolved into the night save for one who entered the building. He stood at the door surveying the interior for a while then walked to the front window wall and stared out into the night. He was immaculately dressed in his army uniform, pants creased and tucked into spit-shined boots, medals and buttons gleaming, badges all in place and a green beret on his head. Slim had just gotten out of the army himself but he didn't need his experience to tell him this guy was special forces – one of the army's trained killers. He had just decamped from an all-night bus but not a thing was mussed or out of place. He stood straight as if he were on the parade ground but projected the feeling of a cat at ease and when he turned back toward Slim, who was wiped out, his face didn't register tired at all. He appeared to be pondering, deciding what to do. He was severely hand-some; his skin was tan and his eyes black and he was in a bus station in Gallup, New Mexico in the dead of night and Slim guessed he was probably Navajo. Without acknowledg-ing Slim as the only other person in the nighttime universe, he sat down in the plastic row a couple of seats away as still as a meditation. Slim could feel that the man was working on something but decided on the basis of two ships passing in the middle of a fluorescent ocean to strike up a conversation.

I just got out. Left every last bit of army stuff in a locker at Fort Sam Houston and walked away. Oh yeah? Did my time. That was enough. Uh huh. Where you headed? Here. On leave? No. Got a couple of days special to do what I'm doing here. I was with a Civil Affairs unit in Panama. It was staffed with doctors, veterinarians and engineers. One of those engineers, a friend of mine, is working now on the reservation. I figure to look him up this morning. Oh yeah? I knew some green berets in Panama. They were involved with the guys who got Che in Bolivia. Is that so. I guess I heard about that. You got family here? Come for a quick visit? For the first time, he turned in his seat and looked right at Slim. I'm here to find a guy. They told me he raped my sister. I'm going to find him quick and cut his balls off. With that, he stood and walked out the door and Slim watched him through the glass cross the yellow glare and disappear into the dark.

7

THE POSSUM

The only way to get to Tasbaponie is by boat and it was dark by the time they arrived. The surf gleamed phosphorescent as they rode in through the waves up onto the sand. A dark skinned man appeared out of the night, helped pull the canoa up out of the surf and said: You stay at my house. Come with me. He was full of stories, advice and admonitions as his wife fed us and set us up for the night but Slim was tired and in retrospect remembered nothing of the barrage of talk except for one thing he said, "You boys watch out for the possum."

Tasbaponie was a single line of thatched or tin-roofed houses set for 100 yards along the strand on the Caribbean coast of Nicaragua. The Mosquito Coast. The people who lived there seemed to Slim at first to be black African but later he could tell by their high cheek bones and their somewhat oriental eyes they were also Miskito Indian. They spoke their own language but they also and usually spoke English. Their connections were to and from the east across the Caribbean to Jamaica rather than west up the rivers, through the rain forest and over the mountains to Spanish speaking Nicaragua. They referred to those Nicaraguans as 'Spaniards'. Slim assumed the blacks arrived as escaped slaves and moved in with the Miskito. Thinking back on those people, Slim thought they were the sweetest, most accommodating people he had ever run into. They were turtle hunters. They fashioned their canoas out of massive logs and barbed harpoon heads out of old files which would embed causing the big turtles to exhaust themselves pulling the canoas so that the men could grab the flippers and haul them aboard.

After a successful hunt, the people would gather on the beach to help drag the turtle past the water line where it would be cut out of its shell, the meat distributed around and the bits and pieces left to the roaming dogs, pigs and chickens. They took care to harvest the famous 'tortoise shell' which is actually the thin, brittle outer layer of the whole shell which they saved for sale by lifting it off with boiling water.

Slim at first pondered the possibilities of slim pickings food wise while he was staying in Tasbaponie with his old friend Dangerous Dan. The village was so isolated and tucked as it was between the sea and a salt water lagoon, it was not a promising spot for agriculture. However, it turned out they lived quite well there. Besides turtle stew and turtle meat balls, they ate hunted meat of 'wildwood pig' (tapir) and deer with fish and breadfruit fried in oil extracted from coconuts, and clams and snails, and shrimp caught with a butterfly net in the lagoon, and always with transported rice and red beans. Dangerous Dan (El Peligroso) was not the dangerous sort who would just as well disembowel you as hug you but rather he was dangerous in the sense that the laws of physics didn't seem to apply in his vicinity. So, for instance, a light bulb might fall from its socket upon his entering a room or a perfectly good seeming chair would collapse under him as he pulled up to the table.

Dangerous Dan was at that time in the Peace Corps, had just been assigned to Tasbaponie and had suggested to Slim that he tag along. Slim was on his way south but didn't think twice about diverting to this side trip and so it was that he was staying in a hut with Dan when things began to heat up. He realized after the first night that the man who met them on the beach and orchestrated their arrival had been expecting them all along and had been waiting for them. His name was Mister Shake/um – not Shakeum or Shake – but Mister Shakeum.

What he told them that first night he undoubtedly repeated as the days went by for he was a wise man and full of advice. The things he had to say were by turns valuable, intriguing or downright bizarre. He told Slim when you get caught in one of those stupid 'pass the bottle' drinking sessions, don't refuse the white lightning, just put the bottle to your mouth, glug your Adam's apple up and down a few times then gasp, smack your lips and pass the bottle on. They'll never know you didn't drink and they will think you are the macho man and worthy of respect. He also emphasized to Slim the importance of paying attention to the moon. He said don't cut poles for your house during the new moon; catch more fish at full moon; and "woman she sick at full moon while others have it at new moon." But he didn't say anything more about the possum and Slim let it slide and gave it no more thought till much later when it hit him what Mister Shakeum had said – "watch out".

Things began to heat up when Valda came by the hut one evening. She said to the dangerous one, "I been watching you and I like your looks. You want to have a woman to mash?" Whatever mashing could be, El Peligroso was up for it, and, before you could ponder the possibilities, they were mashing themselves, or himself, crazy. Valda. Valda Garcia. She could talk as well as she could mash and during the long tropical evenings when they all would be lying in their hammocks in the cabin, she talked her story, talked her life and loves, talked her friends and enemies, talked dirty, coarse, frank, poetic while Slim soaked up that voice coming out of the Tasbaponie dark. She was maybe in her mid-twenties with black skin and long straight hair. She had a nice face and a slim, lithe body. She said she was ¼ Miskito, ¼ Latino and ½ black. She would rap non-stop laughing and jumping out of the hammock and elaborating her stories until she would lose track. She told about challenging a woman from Monkey Point to a public fight. She said, "I'll tell you candid" she needed to "stand up and fight like a woman"; I gave her a "bitch lick" and "bust her ass". She said she loved to grind or mash – that she was just a 'grindin fool' – but in the village she only does it with strangers because the village boys would talk down her reputation. If a man wants to grind, let him get in there and grind and none of that shit foolin' around. The men there, she said, don't like a juicy cunt –

they like it tight and dry and will talk around disparagingly about a juicer the next day. She said the reason she had bred only two children is that while mashing she holds back and lets the man fire first – that way she won't breed. She said that bitch from Monkey Point was bugging her but she had to get a permit for a public fight or they would put her in jail. With a permit and a bikini on, she busted her ass but she kept a knife hidden in her bottoms just in case. She talked about 'obia' and how you had to be careful or your enemies would hang the black magic on you and how she had a lover whose father hated her so he put obia on his son to cause him to fall for a girl from Bluefields and forget Valda. She was a wildcat but an irresistible one and Daniel was smitten. Whatever he was supposed to be doing there in the Peace Corps didn't stand a chance against this love affair.

Slim had been in Tasbaponie long enough and decided to start moving south again. He figured Dan had some limit somewhere to his dangerousness and would burn through Valda probably sooner than later and that would be the end of the story. Before Slim stepped into the canoa to leave, Mister Shakeum met him on the strand to say goodbye and Slim thought to ask what was this all about some possum you said? What man, he replied, you don' know? That Possum. She Valda.

Several months later Slim found himself in a hut in central Panama attending a gathering of Peace Corps volunteers. One was a young lady recently come from Nicaragua. How's Dan? Slim asked. Oh. He just got married. Married? Holy Shit! To somebody maybe named Valda? Yes, that sounds right. You mean legally and officially married? Yep. Well, shiver me timbers and blow me out of the water. Slim needed to sit down and cogitate this one through. How was it possible? Mister Shakeum warned us that very first night. Watch out for the Possum. How did he know she could do something like this. Obia. Obia it had to be. What did she say when talking about obia? He pieced it together. Valda was actually from a village nearby across the lagoon called Wakamba. In the middle of the night lying in your hammock in Tasbaponie you could hear drums from across the lagoon in Wakamba. They said, "That place full of obia. They dance obia all night. Not good people there." Valda had once let drop that her mother was considered a witch woman. In her story about the father who had used obia to get his son away from Valda, she said he had used a love potion. Valda's mother would certainly know how to make a love potion, a love potion strong enough to make an All-American boy from a Republican family in lily-white Minnesota marry the 'grindin fool' Possum and take her out of the Miskito coast to the promised land of the U.S.A.

And that is what he did. Several years later Slim got to Minnesota and heard the final chapter. He met Dangerous Dan's stepfather who was the very opposite of dangerous. He was a judge in the local court. A Republican appointed, self-satisfied, holier-than-thou, well-fed keeper of the moral code. Slim tried to picture him absorbing Valda's telling him candid about giving that Monkey Point woman a bitch lick and busting her ass, and could not conjure it. Or imagining the judge taking in Valda's theory on foreplay (just get in there and grind) or her theory on not breeding (let him fire first). It was all just too hard to imagine. Valda would never hold back. She would always be true to herself, but the judge? The hypocritical son of a bitch probably couldn't sleep all night he'd be so het-up and then take it out on Valda the next day.

From what Slim could piece together, it seemed El Peligroso woke up one morning and said to himself, "What the fuck"? Slim took this to mean that the obia love potion had finally worn off and Daniel woke up as if from a long dream. At about the same time, Valda had had enough of the self-satisfied, holier-than-thou freezing cold life in Dan's home town and wanted to go back to Tasbaponie. Everybody was cordial and threw up their hands and then washed them of the whole affair. Valda had one last demand. Dan took her to the Salvation Army where she loaded up on every summer dress they had on the racks and then bought two large trunks to accommodate them. The Possum was going back to Nicaragua looking like a queen, a different dress for every day of the week. He bought her a plane ticket to Managua, drove her to the airport and that was the last any of us has heard of Valda. Mister Shakeum's Possum.

8

THE BLACK PRINCE

Run! Run for your lives! Earthquake! It's an earthquake! The Black Prince came yelling, running out of the adobe hut. Old Slimshanks sat up in his hammock. It was the middle of a moonless night along the shore of Lake Nicaragua. Wha? What? What the hell? Earthquake? What earthquake? I don't feel anything. As he slid out onto the ground and still didn't feel anything, he realized that was a stupid thing to say. How was he going to catch a tremor asleep in a hammock strung outside among the trees? The Prince might have only been dreaming, however he was still plenty spooked and besides, just offshore was one of a series of volcanoes including the famous Momotombo. While they all milled around telling terremoto stories and waiting for possible aftershocks, the Prince calmed down but refused to go back inside saying those adobe walls were going to crack and crumble and bury him alive. Dangerous Dan nipped inside, dragged out all the bedding and the night passed tremor free under the stars.

The Black Prince was on the run. He had been on the run for a while fleeing the U.S.A., and though he didn't look the type, he had become evasive and fearful. He was African from Angola and was muscular and broad in the chest, of medium height, with a handsome, intelligent face and he spoke perfectly enunciated grammatical English. He had arrived the day before, having made his way through Mexico, Guatemala and El Salvador following a chain of safe houses finally landing him on the doorstep of the Perkins and Dangerous Dan. He said the U.S. government was after him. The C.I.A. was on his tail. His destination, his salvation, was the tiny country of Guyana where he believed Cheddi Jagan would take care of him. This Cheddi Jagan, who Slim had never heard of, was the once and future prime minister of the self-proclaimed socialist republic of Guyana. The Prince explained that Jagan was a Marxist who represented the Indo-Guyanese and who had just been defeated by Forbes Burnham, a Socialist, who represented the Afro-Guyanese. If Cheddi Jagan didn't take care of him, Forbes Burnham certainly would.

So, you ask, who were the people manning these safe houses for him – this chain of contacts south through Central America – keeping him out of the, according to him, clutches of the C.I.A.? They were no other than the Peace Corps. We are not talking about presidential appointees here but rather individual members who were passing him on from one to the next giving him names and addresses to home in on. At this time in the early 70's, while the U.S. government was still looking for light at the end of the tunnel in Vietnam, many Peace Corps volunteers had signed up to make sure the Army didn't get them. They were determinedly anti-war and distrustful of the U.S. while lamenting the obtuseness and stupidity of those in power. This attitude was shared by every Peace Corps member Slim had encountered and though he had recently been in the Army himself, he felt the same way. He had rattled the Army's cage somewhat but not to the extent that they would crucify him and had managed to escape the service with his political opinions intact but with the lowest rank on the list. So, although nobody could hope to verify the amazing story of the Black Prince, he had been adopted and passed along under the rubric of throwing sand into the gears of a government, blind and on the rails to nowhere.

They named him the Prince because he said he was the son of a chieftain of a certain tribe in Angola. Angola at that time was embroiled in a war of independence from Portugal that ultimately led into a vicious and protracted civil war that also served as another proxy war between the U.S.A. and the U.S.S.R. The Soviets were involved, as were the Cubans and the South Africans. The U.S. in its lust to fight the Communist demon around the globe felt it must intervene. Cheddi Jagan and now Forbes Burnham had been thumbing their noses at the U.S. for a while but recently had really been pissing them off by helping to transport Cuban soldiers to Angola. And, according to the U.S., the Black Prince, his father and their tribe were on the wrong side. They had become part of the worldwide Communist threat which the U.S. was committed to eradicate. The Black Prince had been attending an American university on a student visa when he started to run. The exact details were lost in the emotion of his tellings so just why the C.I.A., F.B.I. or any other governmental authority would be bothering to hunt him down remained a mystery. But he was charismatic and convincing and conducted himself like you thought a prince might, so Slim chose to willingly suspend disbelief and support the man.

Let's take him there, said Potter. Where? To Guyana. What the hell are you talking about? Potter was along for the ride. He had hooked up with Slim at his brother's wedding in El Salvador and wanted to join in hitching south through Nicaragua. He was out of an east coast Episcopalian family and was in training to become a priest. He was seriously eccentric and didn't strike Slim as the priestly type. He carried the white celluloid collar in his pocket and once looking for a ride by the roadside as the traffic paid them no mind, he put on the collar hoping that would influence somebody to stop for a man of God. It didn't. The traffic was probably more repelled by his shoulder length unkempt blond hair than attracted to his plastic collar. However, they eventually made their way to Managua and the Black Prince but not before walking through a shabby little village and, it being dinner time, walking into a shabby little establishment with lights on and people inside in search of something to eat. It turned out to be a brothel serving beer and food on the side. It also turned out to be New Year's Eve. Surprise! Surprise! Whoop di doo! It might have been the saddest New Year's Eve on record. They were the only ones there and the women made half-hearted attempts to liven things up by turning on the music and dancing with each other hoping that something in these two male customers might rise to the occasion. It never did. Slim felt somewhat sorry for the women but just couldn't motivate and Potter was sardonic as the man of God trapped in a whorehouse in Nicaragua on New Year's Eve.

Potter was a wild and crazy guy who just happened to be studying theology. He brought a white linen formal jacket to show off the best man at his brother's wedding, and when the bride protested her right to be the star in white, he shrugged and wore it anyway. He had kept a highly irregular pet in a New York City apartment. It was an otter he said that would regularly tear everything in the apartment to pieces, splash and trail water from the half-filled tub all over, shit feces that smelled like fish in the corners, and leave half-eaten chunks of fish to rot on the rugs. He was care-less and care-free and Slim had come to feel this guy was capable of just about anything. So, when he proposed taking the Black Prince to Guyana, Slim said, after what the hell, 'What's the idea?'

Potter had a trust fund to his name. He could call his banker and have the man send a bunch of money. They could take the money and the Black Prince to the Caribbean coast, buy a fishing boat or something with a motor that would float and waltz on down to Guyana. Well, knock me over with a feather, said Slim, just as easy as pie. That's the craziest proposal I've ever heard. Let's do it! I've been in Bluefields and seen the harbor full of boats. We could surely pick up something. Oh, the delightful insanity of it. The ignorance, the innocence, the blissful call to adventure! What a fantastic idea! Let's do it! The absolute idiocy of the idea was out of sight then, beyond their horizon. Slim had now and again puttered about in a row boat; Potter had sailed some in a skipjack off the New Jersey coast; and it just so happens to be 1800 miles straight along the 12oN parallel from Bluefields around the Guajira, by Curaçao, through Grenada and Trinidad to Guyana. And if you hug the coast as they certainly would have to do, knowing nothing about navigation, the miles would stretch considerably longer.

But they didn't look at any maps of course. We are sitting right close to South America and Guyana is right there at the top of the continent. It can't be too far. The absolute adventure of it had them captivated. Potter sent for the money. That is, he tried to. $10,000 should do it, they figured, or not figured at all; just a friendly round number off the tops of their heads. It took days to get a phone call through to Merrill Lynch in N.Y.C. Crackled connections; international operators; mistranslations, misunderstandings; your party is not in the office right now, may I have him call you back? And even then the family banker was not too enthusiastic about sending ten thou into the never-never land in which he assumed Managua to be located. However, Potter wrangled him, yelling into the phone something about chicken shit, and the money did come - $10,000 at your service in the Banco Central de Nicaragua. But even that transaction took two more days and when they divvied it into various national currencies and travelers checks and dollars which are good anywhere, and then came up for air and looked around, the Black Prince was gone. Gone. Disappeared. No trace of him and no word of where or why.

They waited around a few more days to see if he would turn up then decided he was gone for good. Slim recalibrated and decided to start moving south again, so Potter stuffed those 10,000 notes into a bag, took it and himself to the Managua airport and rode the 707 back to N.Y.C.

Many moons passed before Slim wised up enough to plumb the depths and measure the width of their folly in fomenting this stupendous plan. Perhaps they were saved from their own magnetic attraction to the poles of folly by the Black Prince himself. Did he calculate the percentages and review the cast of characters and decide he was better off on his own? Perhaps so, because Slim was privy to one more glimpse of him before he disappeared forever. A glimpse - not really – perhaps a shadow of a glimpse it was. It happened at the Costa Rica – Panama border crossing where Slim stood in line waiting to get passed through. The process was slower than usual. It was tropical hot and he was feeling sluggish and weary but he perked up overhearing two customs guys conversing off to one side. One said to the other, "What about that guy? Que hombre, eh? Yeah he sure was and we probably shouldn't have let him through. But what a story he told. Incredible." Then they were interrupted and dragged off to investigate someone, but Slim knew. He shivered a little with the secret knowledge. He just knew it had to be the Black Prince they were discussing and that he had gone through the border ahead of Slim. The Black Prince was

one border closer to his goal and Slim inwardly smiled and
wished him Godspeed.

{ 9 }

PISSED OFF

There is a certain etiquette that pertains to a public urinal. Etiquette might not be quite the right word. Let's say instead that a certain mode of behavior reigns therein. If you have no choice and all the other urinals are occupied, you would step in next to someone already there. Otherwise, you would want to leave at least one empty space between you and a man already in place. Once there and unzipped, you stare resolutely at the wall in front of you or down at your penis in hand. You do not look to either side thus avoiding eye contact and you do not usually start conversations during the process. The bigger, farther from home and more forbidding the city housing this urinal, the more pertinent these unstated rules become. For instance, if you happen to find yourself in one in Grand Central Station in N.Y.C., you would certainly want to follow the guidelines and vacate as fast as possible. When it so happens that someone deviates from the mode, red flags begin to flutter. It may be that this someone is just an innocent or a free spirit and of no consequence but more likely it means trouble of one kind or another. Trouble, of course, is only as you define it. One man's trouble is another's good time. It doesn't suit my purpose here to go into all the possibilities but, all things considered, what's likely to come down in a public urinal is not likely to be pleasant.

Old Slimshanks was not actually considering these sociologies when he stepped out of the merciless sun into a dim public urinal in Coatzacoalcos. When you are traveling and wandering around a strange city, a sometimes major question often balloons – where can you take a piss? The spectacular city and popular tourist destination of Cuzco in Peru used to be known by the cognoscenti as 'shit city' because of the uncivilized nature of visiting Indians coming into town from the surrounding wilds. Not knowing what else to do, they would piss and shit in every nook and cranny of the city. Slim, however, didn't like the idea of pissing into crannies so coming upon a public urinal was always a pleasant surprise and bolstered his faith in city planners.

There was no one in this one he could see as his eyes adjusted away from the hammering sunlight. The set-up there was, not uncommon in Mexico, a long single trough running the length of the back wall with drainage holes bored into it every couple of feet. As Slim settled to his task, he heard somebody come in behind him. He wasn't going to pay him any mind or acknowledge his presence but when the man took his place right beside Slim with all the rest of the trough open to him, those red flags unfurled in the wind and his heart went into overdrive. And when the man, after a minute's silence, hissed, "Psst, gringo," Slim feared the worst, and when he turned his head to look, the man was standing there with his penis in his left hand and a pistol in his right waving in the air in front of his face. All other thoughts being crowded out of his head, Slim could only think, "So this is way its going to end? Shot to death in a urinal in Coatzacoalcos?" He pictured his gravestone with its terse message – Pissed Off In Coatzacoalcos.

The man was young, about Slim's age, and to Slim's eye didn't appear to be the murdering type. But he was standing there pissing heartily into the trough while waving the pistol in his direction. Not knowing what else to do, Slim just said, "Buenos dias." The man replied, "Quieres comprarla?" Do you want to buy this pistol? Wouldn't you like to purchase this sweet, little pistola? By all that's sweet in life, the guy was actually offering that pistol up for sale! He wanted Slim to buy the thing. Slim stammered and mumbled, "No, no, muchas gracias. Muy amable. That's very friendly of you. Muchas gracias. Adios" and hied out of there into the merciful Mexican sun.

{ **10** }

ISLAND FEVER

It so happened when Slim boated into Ailigandí they were gearing up for a big fiesta. Ailigandí is one of the San Blas islands where the Kuna have been one of the few Native American tribes to have not only survived the European onslaught but also prospered. The islands form an archipelago along the Caribbean coast of Panama and the Kuna are ostensibly Panamanian but actually govern themselves. Since this coast comprised part of the 'Spanish Main', perhaps the Kuna survived the depredations of the Conquistadores and the pirates by fleeing the islands and staying out of sight in the adjacent jungle, and perhaps their hitherto immutable rule of never letting strangers stay on the islands after sundown helped keep their society and bloodlines intact. Either way, they are a wealthy and prosperous people whose monetary income gets converted into hammered gold ornaments the women hang from their ears or around their necks.

For many years they had contracts with the U.S. military to provide workers on their bases in the Canal Zone – menial work like mopping barracks and washing dishes and cleaning up in the mess halls. They were quiet and self-effacing and they seemed to do this work happily, probably because they were paid U.S. minimum wage, a fortune for menial work in Panama. Consequently great quantities of money found its way over those years into the islands. So much so that a young pair of these 'primitive Indians' Slim had befriended and given a mess-hall-napkin-scrawled address showed up one day at Slim's father's Madison Ave N.Y.C. office and invited themselves to dinner in the suburbs.

The San Blas islands are small – there are a half-dozen main islands and a bunch of smaller ones. They could be measured in meters across rather than miles and every square inch is occupied or utilized. The houses of bamboo and thatch or tin roofed are crammed cheek by jowl right to the water's edge with meandering pathways between. Slim was headed south to Colombia via San Blas and had gotten as far as Ailigandí to await a further ride with the coconut traders. When he stepped onto the island he could feel all was abuzz. It was such that he was walking into one of the periodic blow-outs when the whole island participates in celebrating the cutting of a girl's hair. This is a major milestone in the life of a Kuna girl. It's symbolic of the passage into womanhood and the child-bearing years. Kuna girls run free and careless throughout the island with their long hair unfettered down their backs while their older sisters and mothers all have their hair cut very short and keep a red and yellow shawl about their heads. The actual hair-cutting ceremony was a private and family affair but what Slim was caught up in was the excuse the people used to stage a massive party.

Once Slim realized what was going on and followed the

crowd to the large meeting hall in the center of the island, he began to ruminate on this question of long hair vs short hair. This was no small question coming as it did in the flux of the hippie revolution during the early 1970s, the uniting symbol worldwide being long hair – unruly hair. Did the cutting of a teenage girl's hair in the San Blas have anything to say about the reality of the generally accepted symbolism around buzz cuts vs shags; art vs law; order vs disorder; efficiency vs do your own thing; marching in time vs strolling to your own tune; neat vs slovenly? The list goes on – the Spartans vs the Athenians; the Romans and the Gauls; the Prussians and the French; the Mods and the Rockers; The Dopers and the Ropers; the Hippies and the Straights. One side lets their hair go and the other keeps it trimmed. What did this have to do with Kuna women, mused Slim, as things began to heat up around him. First of all, he knew these women were the core and strength of their society. They maintained the resilience and cultural continuity of their people and were inherently conservative. Law and order, in the real, base-line sense of it, were absolute necessities in such places as their bee-hive-like islands. They had to keep things working efficiently and everybody had to march to the same tune or the villages would self destruct. So it fit in to this reasoning according to Slimshanks, that once you came of age you had to forsake your careless childhood freedoms as well as your beautiful but unruly hair.

Slim could muse along all he wanted about historical parallels and such but he was unprepared for what hit him next. Inside the meeting house were placed two large dugout canoes, one at each end, and behind the canoes arrayed against the walls were benches full of women at one end and men at the other. In the canoes was chicha. It had been brewing for weeks in preparation for this event. It was made from corn, sugar cane juice and cacao beans. The corn had been chewed by the women and spit into large tinajas. The cane had the juice squeezed out of it which was then added, and the chocolate beans were crushed and thrown in on top. The whole concoction hissed and bubbled for three weeks before being dumped into the two dugouts. Chewing and spitting sounds uncouth and unhygienic but they worry not about such concerns. They are looking for alcohol, and to get corn to ferment you need to do something to it in order to mobilize the starch into sugar. You can do this by sprouting and grinding the corn or, better yet, your teeth and the enzymes in your saliva will take care of the problem for you. Sugar cane juice, on the other hand, is a potential alcohol powerhouse and needs no help from you to ferment. Cacao adds caffeine and its own kind of chocolate magic to the brew. Slim soon caught on to the idea in progress – there was no doubt everybody was to get as intoxicated as humanly possible and some were on course to leave their earthly moorings completely.

The four honchos who were leading the way had started the binge by giving each other rapid fire shots across the boat, dipping and pouring somewhere near each other's mouths. Slim supposed these four were the closest male relatives to the girl getting shorn. Another group of men, perhaps increasingly distant relatives, were standing off to the side and were attended to by six or seven runners. These guys were receiving full gourds of chicha from the runners, whooping and grunting and doing a mincing circle dance before downing the chicha and handing back the empty for another run. Another group of runners were, at the same time, scooping and bringing totumas to the hoi polloi seated around the outside, men first as the women watched and waited.

The runners wore headbands of red, yellow and blue parrot feathers, and necklaces, arm and ankle bracelets made from a loose collection of what looked like small animal bones. They pranced and jangled back and forth ferrying chicha to all and every. Slim sat and waited his turn. It was dark brown, vile, textured somewhat slimy and smelled like vinegar but he chugged his portion as fast as possible trying not to taste anything as it went down. While the runners were passing out chicha, two other evil magicians were dispensing tobacco smoke to further intoxicate the multitude. They had rolled tobacco leaves into cigars many inches thick and three feet long and were bouncing along the lines of attendees blowing smoke under each nose. To do this, they put the lighted end in their mouths, puffed their cheeks mightily and blew. With the cigar end under your nose, you were expected to inhale deeply which Slim did only once, feeling himself to be more fragile by the minute, while everyone else sucked those cigars down to the size of thimbles before making way for the next. By the time Slim had put away four rounds of that chicha del diablo, he figured those guys in the center had put away twenty, and, as things began to cloud

over, he thought maybe he was dealing with a bunch of su-
perheroes here.

As he was pondering his escape route, those guys were not
only still standing but also hadn't even gone anywhere yet to
piss. "Who are those guys?" He kept cracking himself up repeating this immortal movie line as who knows how many
hours had passed and the chicha and smoke were still flow-
ing. Bedlam it had become when Slim stumbled out of there.
Virtually everyone in the entire village was completely shitfaced. There were people singing, laughing, fighting, vomiting, bear-hugging and lying on the ground. By this time, the
women had caught up with the men and were mixed in to
the general scrum. Slim, looking to get back to home base
or alternatively find a safe buoy to moor to, was meandering around the maze of pathways trying to conjure a land-
mark when an old woman came out of one of the thatched
houses and grabbed him by the wrist. She seemed fiercely
strong and, as she pulled him toward her door, she grabbed
his crotch with her other hand.

Now Slim had been around on the islands long enough to
know these old women ran the show. Arbiters of correct behavior, they were always primed to pounce on anyone they
deemed to be out of line, out of tune or just plain foolish.
In the early mornings when Slim might walk about waking
himself, the old women would be out sweeping the sand in
front of their doorways or sitting on a bench there smoking
a pipe. Their hair now grown out again long and gray, their
shirts off and their breasts hanging to their waists looking
like brown paper bags stuck to their chests, they would call

out to him and to each other laughing and joking, and he would understand nothing but know they were on to him. They enforced the rules but had attained a status themselves allowing them to do as they wished, and now one of them had him by the balls and was pulling him into her house. Judging her by comparison to his own people he would have said she was about 75 years old but taking into account anthropological differences he figured she was probably only 60. She had a grip of steel and as she urged him forward with both hands Slim thought this could only mean one thing. It was free play time on the island and she had captured a prize, a 'mergi' even, and she was evidently hoping to ride his cowboy. He could have been amused by this or even annoyed but he found himself to be momentarily terrified. She was strong but after all she was an old woman; he wrenched free of her and bolted, hearing her complaining to his back as he disappeared.

After passing the night on somebody's earthen floor, it mattered not whose, and waking to chanting and drumming which after some concern he realized was not coming from inside his own head, Slim reflected the best thing that happened to him amidst all this revelry was to have vomited – multiple times, losing count. His body had rescued his sorry excuse of a person and saved him from an unreasonable share of misery. He followed the chanting back to the meeting house and - "Who ARE those guys?" – in disbelief he saw the leading troopers were still going. The giant cigars were still circulating and the canoes were an unending fount of chicha. They had been at it all night and were headed on into the next day and, as it turned out, also into the third day when the actual hair cutting ceremony took place. By that stage all the women were deeply involved: dancing, laughing, cackling, falling down, and trying to get Slim to dance any time he hove into view.

'Those guys' eventually began to crash like ancient trees in the forest succumbing one by one face first into the sand and, as the island lapsed into rest and recovery, Slim assessed what had been going on. He thought these people really had things figured right. They were conservative; they were law abiding; they hadn't fallen into alcoholism and whoredom like so many Native American tribes; they kept a tight rein on each other. But where there are people there are politics and where there are politics there is conflict. It is inevitable within any group so close and so constricted that there arise jealousy, envy, cruelty and hatred. The question becomes how to deal with these inevitabilities so they don't metastasize out of control and blow the community apart. Their answer seemed to be, instead of a blow up lets have a blow out.

They stage periodic, purposeful, community wide intoxications. Unleash the Lord of Misrule for a few days and let it all happen. Get your revenge; attempt to beat hell out of that s.o.b.; brawl and bawl and roll in the dirt; fuck your neighbor's wife while your wife is you know not where doing you know not what; grab a 'mergi' with your iron fingers and get him to fuck you – all is permissible and forgivable because you are too drunk to know what you're doing. You are too far gone to actually hurt anyone or to be held accountable for anything, and grudges and tensions have been worked through so that when the fog clears everything is forgotten and life gets back to the pleasant everyday. Slim thought about this and concluded the Puritans would have benefited mightily if they had been blown off course and landed in San Blas instead of Massachusetts. Instead of getting all bound up and wound up with no way out and pasting scarlet letters on the prettiest girl in town and sallying forth to kill some Indians, they could have been singing and dancing and fucking each other two or three times every year.

A few days later Slim hopped a ride with the coconut traders and boated out of San Blas south to Colombia. In the relative quiet of a cheap hotel room he opened his pack and spread things out with the intention to clean and reorganize. He came to a contact lens case and popped it open. It was 2"x2" small, made from white plastic with two dimples inside just the size of the lenses. The lenses were gone. They were from another life and had been dropped on him as a member of a college football team. He rarely used them and probably hadn't checked on them in weeks, but he conjured a scenario explaining their disappearance and couldn't help but smile.

While in Ailigandí Slim had been hanging out in the house of an extended family of ten people. That is to say, he hung his hammock alongside everyone else and propped his pack nearby against a pole. He also ate his meals with them, so even though they were always in and out he got to know all the family members. One was an intriguing young man who, we could say, was 'challenged' in some way; he had characteristics of an 'idiot savant'. He couldn't communicate directly but he was always smiling at Slim, and laughing and showing off his collections and arrangements of beautiful objects. Shells, feathers, colored stones, butterfly wings, bird eggs and such, he would arrange them into patterns that apparently had great meaning for him.

Slim looked further and discovered that his fingernail clippers were also gone, a thing that is a dime a dozen to us but when looked at with new eyes could be considered a miraculous object. Slim was sure now of his vision of the boy going through his pack while the island rocked and checking out every single thing. He neatly and carefully replaced everything but when he popped open the little contact lens box and saw the two perfect tiny domes of green tinted glass, he couldn't possibly resist their allure. The fingernail clippers were indeed wonderful but the green tinted lenses were a treasure beyond thought, beyond dreams. Slim enjoyed the image as he repacked, figuring he knew where the boy would keep his new treasures. He had shown Slim a box he had made out of the beak of a macaw. The two parts of the beak were hinged with a piece of leather at the back and secured at the front with a thong. A tight little beak box, just the right size to house the two lenses. Slim could picture the boy secreting the beak and going to it now and again to admire and handle them, and he thought – that boy will remember my visit long after the lady of the iron fingers has forgotten.

11

THE SWAGGER STICK

When Slim walked off the boat onto he docks of Turbo he was feeling grumpy about coconuts. Grumpy and lumpy. He knew about the miraculous nature of the coco tree and its fruit. How it populated tropical beaches around the globe. How a nut could fall ripe into the water and end up sprouting in the sand of Bora Bora, thousands of miles away. How you could scramble up the trunk like those Kuna boys and throw down a couple of green ones, take a machete and lop the top off one, drink the cool, sweet milk and then scrape out the inside with a piece of coco shell and it was coconut crème. How the flesh of a mature nut could be dried in the sun becoming copra to be kept for eating later or trade. How you could crack open dozens of nuts and fill a pot with the flesh, add water and boil over a fire of palm branches until a thick layer of oil bubbled on the surface and now you could pan fry your plátanos. And how the coconut was the unit of commerce throughout the San Blas. It was 1973 and each coco could be sold for one U.S. nickel. They were mostly sold to Colombian boatmen out of Turbo. These marineros who were mainly black, motored empty north through the islands and loaded their open wooden freighters with coconuts as they wended back south When they were packed mounded to the gunnels they headed home, so Slim begged a ride and the capitán said OK but you'll have to ride on the coconuts. Slim considered himself to be a rugged individualist, a road or sea warrior, and sleeping on coconuts sounded just like another adventure to him.

Slim might have been some kind of warrior but he occasionally exhibited behavior that was usually associated with damn fools. He was headed to South America and figured that to get there out of Panama he would merely stroll through the Darién. It wasn't far and he knew the British army had just famously headed through on an advertising junket for Range Rover. He would follow their wheel ruts, but what he hadn't heard was that they abandoned the project deep in and had to be helicoptered out of there. So of course Slim, the mighty road warrior, terrified himself when he realized he had no idea and was indeed lost in the jungle until he stumbled on a Chocó encampment. Chocó, where the women wore no clothes except when they went to town and put on brassieres discarded by the latinas and hip wraps so as not to excite the rubes. The Chocó put him up for the night and pointed him back to the Canal and so onto the coconuts for two nights and days, coming into Turbo where the broad river pours sweet water far out into the sea and the crew, stripped and holding onto ropes, jumped in to rinse off the sweat, grime and salt before hitting home. Slim watched as one tucked his long penis like a hunk of garden hose between his thighs and hopped and skipped that way along the deck and off the stern. Why he did that, Slim couldn't figure. Perhaps he was just modest or perhaps he didn't want his penis banging against his thighs as he ran.

Be that as it may, sleeping on coconuts isn't conducive to feeling jaunty and Slim was somewhat grumpy walking into the maelstrom that was Turbo. He realized that his grudge against coconuts would soon enough dissolve into a story and besides, he was now in Colombia where there was no customs man to be seen or found. In fact, the town, from the docks on outward, came at him like a runaway train – no one in control and headed down the rails looking for trouble. Slim had never been and has never been since in such a wild town. Watch your pockets, watch your back and pray he contemplated as he entered the first bar he came to, with the idea of washing down the sea salt and coconut fur that was clinging like a crustacean in his throat.

The place had swinging saloon doors just like old western movie saloons and, honest to God, no sooner had he sat down than some crazed cowboy all booted and spurred barreled his horse right through the doors, skidded on the smooth wooden floor, reined his beast viciously into a pirouette and blasted and yodeled his way back into the street. Slim's initial reaction was awe that this archetypical movie scene could happen in real life. But after things calmed down and Slim was feeling quenched and sipping his second beer, he thought, was this a case of real life or life imitating art? He decided even these berserk Colombians in Turbo had seen all the old Hollywood westerns over the years. After all, Hollywood had been sending horses through saloon doors since

1930. This nut-case of a cowboy had surely watched Randolph Scott do that and had just been waiting his chance to buy or steal that pair of silver dollar spurs and put them on for show time.

The streets of Turbo were packed with people and horses and Japanese motor bikes and noise and dust and drunks and prostitutes and campesinos come in out of the bush and coconut sailors and vendors charring meat by the roadside or selling fruit or making licuados out of a pile of fruit and a blender plugged into random stray electrical wires. This was some concatenation of humanity. Every one of these humans was on the make somehow and energy was being generated and dissipated like wind from an unknown place. Slim got himself a room demarked by cardboard walls in an establishment leaning out over the main street where apparently the party just kept on revving all night. Even in his coconutted sleep deprived condition, he awakened now and again throughout the night wondering about his cardboard walls and listening to periodic gunshots interspersed with existential howlings, drunken singing, men fighting in the street and very loud and non-stop cumbia. Welcome to Colombia it was and as Slim was cogitating the possibility that the whole country was like this, he resolved to split town in the morning and find out.

The next day he was peering down over the edge of the road into a sheer drop 500 feet to the river and thought he was about to die in this miserable little bus driven by what appeared to be a couple of teenagers who were clearly drunk and having a fine old time careening the thing as fast as possible along the twisting road carved into the valley wall, following the mighty Magdalena into the interior. They pulled off periodically into roadside caravanserai with no word to the passengers and threw down another glass of aguardiente with, it seemed, the intention of enlivening this dull trip a wee bit more. Maybe everybody is a cowboy in this country, thought Slim. In the figurative sense anyway. Consequences be damned. Hop on that bull and ride him through the fences and onto the road and full speed ahead!

He'd been hitchhiking his way through Central America but he'd thought to bus out of Turbo not feeling too confidant in the ride possibilities. However, while wondering why he was still alive on this bus, he figured hitching didn't seem too risky after all. Anybody in Colombia in those days driving a personal automobile in the country was likely to be a member of the upper class – that is, the land owning class – a terrateniente, a patron – and one of these guys stopped for Slim, took a hold of him and proceeded to educate him in all things Colombian. He told Slim Colombia was the most beautiful and bountiful piece of the entire planet occupied by the worst people. They have saturated this land with their own blood since even before the Spaniards arrived. The Chibcha practiced ritual slaughter and offered up human blood to their voracious gods and the gold haunted and bloodthirsty conquistadores felt compelled by their god to sacrifice the sacrificers. The slaughter has proceeded almost non-stop and la violencia lives with us even today. He said, watch out for yourself but think what beauty we live in. Here the Andes divide into two mountain chains creating broad fertile valleys with majestic rivers. We have two sea coasts. The Costa Caribe where the Sierra Nevada de Santa Marta rises straight from the ocean to almost 6000 meters and there are timid people who live up there lost in the clouds. There are Spanish colonial cities on the coast; there are Indian encampments hidden in the jungle; there are birds and animals of the tropics and of the high Sierras. There are birds here from the north and birds from the south. Colombia is the meeting house of the Americas. There are birds so beautiful, he said, they will dazzle your eyes. There are towns so lonely and cold in the mountains so as to make you forget your way. On the other side of the Andes there are savannas so vast they roll all the way to the Amazon.

He was proud of his country; he was proud of himself. He had the demeanor, thought Slim, of one who owned the earth he walked on and all those on it. He was strong and opinionated and when he let Slim off, he gave him a keepsake. It was a switch made from a slim supple branching laced about with leather thong alternating natural and black and he said keep this at your side for luck and use it against thieves, vicious dogs and bad women. As Slim sat beside the road holding his new swagger stick, he thought does that wonderful old man actually swat his women with one of these? He couldn't imagine: probably just the requisite macho posture showing itself.

That switch did bring good luck. Slim hadn't found it necessary to use it on any of the three designated targets but it led him into the orbit of a young caballero and his Paso Fino horses. There is genuine cowboy country in northeast Colombia called Antioquia. This caballero dressed the part and confessed his heart's desire was to have a pair of real fancy boots from Texas and maybe Slim could send him some one day. Learning this caused Slim to change his perspective on the dude who liked to ride through saloon doors in Turbo. The caballero and his classmates liked to prance their hot-blooded horses up and down the high street through town, reining them in and spurring at the same time causing their necks and tails to be arched, their heads held high and their front legs to beat out a high dance while they swiveled sideways back and forth down the street. One day the caballero said: You ride my horse back. I'll take Benicio's and she and I will go around the valley and we'll met you back at the ranch. Slim said: What about Benicio? Benicio was his foreman, his mayor domo. He is bueno para caminar, he said, and rode off with his lady. They started off and once out of sight Slim wasn't feeling democratic about playing the mountie while Benicio trotted alongside, so he said: Hop on buddy. Benicio grinned mightily and they rode home double. Slim told him: Where I come from, everybody rides.

It was a time when hippies from all over the planet were wandering around Colombia and, like bees to a hive, they homed to Río La Miel where the mushrooms grew near cow patties in the pastures along the river decorated with groves of giant bamboo arcing and dancing against the sky. Slim visited, tasted the honey and came away sensitized in various strange ways. One way was that the beauty of all women overwhelmed him and left his heart feeling naked. It was in that condition he arrived in Cali.

The only thing he knew about the city of Cali he had learned from a girl he had run into in Panama. She was vivacious and pretty and told him she was in Panama on a contract working as a prostitute. He said well, well what's that about? She said she was from Cali, Colombia and lots of women from Cali come short term to Panama to make some money in order to set up back home. The international conglomeration of lonely men there presented an unlimited business opportunity. It's all right, she said, I don't mind too much. So Slim found himself sitting on a bench in the central plaza in Cali watching a parade of pulchritude the likes of which he had never dreamed. The place had more dazzling females per square meter than could be thought possible. They had it on and they knew it. They dressed it; they walked it; they perfumed and eye shadowed it; and why and wherefore Slim could not figure, but it reduced him to a quivering pulp of raw male. It was in this state of mind and body that Slim left town heading south and dropped into a small museum tucked away into some woods a few miles out of town.

He browsed for a while by himself until a crowd of kids came in together. Teenagers, perhaps a class trip, and in the midst of their gabbling, he detected hesitant Spanish in an American accent. She was an exchange student doing a junior year abroad. Slim engaged her and she was happy to talk American and receive advice. She looked younger than she was – seemed naïve, bland, wearing braces, still really a little girl in the peculiar way of midwesterners who grow up slow. While they were talking, another girl moved close, listening. Slim was struck with the thought – this is the most beautiful girl I have ever seen in my life. She would probably be the same age as the American girl, a junior in high school, 17 more or less, but the contrast between the two couldn't have been greater. This girl was already a woman. Slim could see it, he could feel it, he knew it and he couldn't take his eyes off her. She wanted to speak to him and started off with a few hesitant English words until Slim assured her they could talk Spanish. She wore no make-up. She had café au lait skin and brown eyes that looked steadily and openly right at him. It seemed to him there was so little artifice in this girl that he might see right through her eyes into her soul. She didn't flirt with him; she knew no feminine wiles; she just soaked him up and asked him straight out if he would come back to Cali and be her lover. Incredible, he flashed, she's 17 and she's obviously a virgin and she's looking at me with those eyes, pools of faith and trust and desire, and he replied, do you feel yourself ready to be loved by a man? He thought he might drown in those eyes when she just said, "Si." He felt his insides cave in. He was smitten. Struck by lightning. Fell in love so fast it was frightening. What should he do? What could he do? All is fair in love and war. Take her back to Cali and love her to pieces. But then what? She is only 17. But this is an extraordinary person. You can't pass this up. She's asking you. She wants you to love her as a man and she's not proposing a teenage puppy affair. He stood in turmoil feeling she had pierced his heart with an arrow and she quietly watched and waited. A 17 year old girl of the most exquisite beauty possessing such faith and confidence and he looked at her and didn't touch her and told her she had put an arrow in his heart that would never come out and praised her courage, her strength and her beauty and said, "I must go," and, feeling like one who had won the grand prize against impossible odds but turned it down, walked away bereft and lonelier than any cloud.

Years have meandered by for Old Slim and he has never forgotten this girl – he never learned her name – and occasionally he revisits his decision. He usually starts out talking to himself saying, you fool, you should have gone with her. No red-blooded man would have refused that offer. But as he works his way through the reasons and seasons again, he always arrives at the same place and walks away again.

12

ECHA LO

If you are traveling south on the Pan-American Highway coming out of Ecuador into Peru, the land seems to have configured and conformed to the political boundaries. It seemed to Old Slimshanks in his travels that it was a rare occasion when you could distinguish the landscape of one country from the next after crossing a border line, but the lush green of Ecuador immediately gives way to sand and stone in coastal Peru. The culprit is the Peru Current carrying cold Antarctic water north along the coast along with its associated dry air. There is no hope of any rain coming in off the ocean to the west and the Andes to the east collect all the water thermalling out of the jungle to send it all back down the Amazon. This phenomenon culminates further south just across the border with Chile in the Atacama which is reputed to be the driest place on the planet. The Peru Current cuts west at the continental bulge that is Ecuador allowing the Ecuadorians to benefit from a warm current coming from the north.

The landscape changes dramatically and so do the people. As Slim hitched his way south along the Peruvian coast, he was caught off guard by the hostility of the locals. Adults staring, sometimes open mouthed; kids giggling; guys yelling from passing cars, "Gringo!"; children scuttling into doorways to tell their mothers, "Mira al gringo." He stopped into a local eaterie for lunch and noticed quite a few tiny red hot peppers – 'ají diablo' – interspersed in his plate of rice and chicken. He looked toward the kitchen door and glimpsed quickly as they pulled back out of sight a couple of young faces grinning and watching to see if he would burn up or be reduced to a puddle of gasping and choking gringo. He furtively pocketed the ají while pretending to be hugely enjoying the meal and afterwards strolled to the kitchen to compliment the chef while suggesting their arroz con pollo could perhaps use a bit more pepper.

However, the behavior of these people was so unlike that of the Ecuadorians in whose company he had just been for weeks, that he was discomfited and kept checking in any reflective surface to see if he hadn't recently sprouted horns. He was thinking about the family who had picked him up in Ecuador and invited him to stay in their house in Quito. A fresh bed in their son's room, a shower, free run of the house – the level of generosity and trust touched and amazed him. The parents left him alone in the house with their teenage daughter. She invited him into her bedroom to show him some of her treasures. It was all so innocent and friendly and trusting. He wondered what parents in the U.S.A. would pick up a total stranger on the road and leave him in their house alone with their teenage daughter. None he could think of. It seemed to be a measure of the power of culture –

all the Ecuadorians he had met were the same open and generous people.

These Peruvians, on the other hand, on their strip of desert north of Lima were of a remarkably different ilk, but he did run into a quota of friendly people and just down the highway he jumped into the wildest hitchhike of his career. It was a 56 Chevy station wagon that pulled up as he begged a ride on the edge of the highway. Most of the paint had been scoured off by the wind and sand and the side panels and fenders had been rusted by the ocean salt. The inside had been scoured by other phenomena down to bare metal. There was no hint of the fabrics, cardboard or plastics that had decorated the interior as it rolled out of the factory. The pull-down back cargo door and window were gone leaving it open to the wind and exhaust. The driver was a middle-aged uncle (tío) and his crew, a 12 year old nephew (sobrino). Immediately Tío informed Slim the gas tank was empty and they had no money so he needed to fork over some cash for gasoline. It was useless to try and explain that the reason he was hitching instead of riding buses, airplanes or trains was because his funds were limited and he had a long way to go, so he handed over the equivalent of one dollar. With that, Tío had Sobrino put about ½ gallon into the tank and the rest into one liter plastic soda bottles while he lifted the hood and peered inscrutably into the motor works.

The ½ gallon got them out of town where Tío stopped and stationed Sobrino on the front bumper with one of those bottles full of gasoline in his hand. The hood was propped open with a stick that was evidently kept for this purpose and tied down against the wind with a length of cord, and off they went onto the coastal highway – the only highway in northern Peru. The desert there comes down to the edge of the Pacific and is characterized by extensive dune action. The dunes come in waves along the coast, 15 feet, 25 feet, some 50 feet high, and the road rides roller coaster fashion up and down over the sand. This topography was the star actor in the play put on by Tío and his nephew at which Slim was agog as the sole audience member. The two were a troupe that had obviously practiced its parts and done this before.

When the wagon commenced to cough and hesitate, foretelling the departure of the last drop of gasoline, Tío stuck his head out the window and yelled into the wind, "Echa lo!" Sobrino, holding on with one hand in front of the half-raised hood, then began dribbling gas out of the bottle slowly into the open mouth of the carburetor and Tío floored it. The decrepit Chevy boomed to the crest of the next dune where Sobrino stopped pouring and Tío shut off the ignition. They coasted down the far side, Tío staying away from any brake and yelling at any slow moving auto-behemoths to get out of his way while weaving around them so as to get as far up the next slope as possible before, at momentum's last gasp, yelling, "Echa lo!" and bombarding uphill again. This roller coaster routine continued for several miles occasionally stopping at the edge of the next precipice to pass Sobrino his next liter. He seemed to be not necessarily enjoying his fuming ride on the front bumper but prideful of his role in the family business. Not only agog was Slim but also horrified at all the direful possibilities that could befall this boy, but he counseled himself to just sit tight and hold on when it began to dawn that this actually was a business venture he was participating in.

Along this coast the roller coaster series of dunes periodically gives way to an open level bench usually created by the outwash of a river coming off the mountains. In these spots were located famous archeological sites such as Chan Chan and the Moche Pyramids and where today's towns are situated along the ocean's edge. As they came rocketing off the last dune down into the outskirts there would be people standing on the apron of the highway usually next to a pile of bags or boxes. Tío stopped for one and then another and as they piled in with their stuff they handed him a small wad of paper notes. He then pulled into the town gas station and traded the fresh money for a couple more gallons. Sobrino, knowing the deal, pulled out the stick, slammed down the hood and hopped in beside Slim. Tío was now ebullient, singing and cracking jokes and taking on more passengers. More passengers and more luggage, now being tied to the roof of the old wagon, and more money yielding more gasoline until by the fourth stop the tank runneth over, the sign Tío had apparently been waiting for, intimating by his loud whoop that there indeed was a God in heaven.

Slim now understood that so ran the wheels of commerce in that zone: if you could scrounge up any old vehicle you could make a payday trucking or bussing people and/or their cargo back and forth between the cities of Trujillo and Chimbote or probably anywhere else on the Peruvian coast. The markets were in the cities where people traveled to sell or buy and commercial service either didn't exist or was too expensive. Slim observed their relationship to the Sol notes they grudgingly passed over to Tío. The riders invariably kept a handful crumpled up in a closed fist and when Tío straightened them out to count, Slim could see this money was tight. It had been scrunched in so many hands that it was soiled, faded and tattered beyond recognition but it still bought gasoline and all other economic lubricants that kept the country from grinding to a stop.

By the time they were on the last leg coming into Chimbote, the 56 Chevy was wallowing with an inconceivable load of people and stuff. The stuff included a crate of chickens, one goat tied across the hood, an entire stalk of bananas, and a random assortment of boxes and burlap bags. As they rolled into town, the only place Slim had ever seen pelicans promenading in the streets like sacred cows and black vultures perched rank and file along the roof tops, Tío was in the catbird seat and had plenty of gas to do the whole thing over again back to home. Sobrino was grinning and laughing and pointing out the sights to Slim as they had escaped the crush of bodies and bags and were riding side by side on the back bumper.

13

THE GREAT BUTTERFLY CAPER

Roberto, Roberto! Venga. Ven acá! No seas pendejo, Roberto. Come on. Come here. Don't be some worthless pubic hair dingle. Join us. It was the mayor of Macusani with his usual cronies sitting on the terrace of the only bar in town looking for any wind-fall amusement that might come their way. Slim groaned considering the prospects of the next few hours.

Macusani was a small, cold, dusty town located at the high point on one of the roads from Titicaca to Amazonia in southern Peru. That put it on the Altiplano at 11,000 feet where the wind roiled the dust around the mostly one-story houses huddled together as if for companionship in the vast openness on top of the world. The road through Macusani was the only way available to vehicular traffic in and out of Slim's temporary home downslope on the Amazon side of the Altiplano, so he had been waylaid by the mayor several times previously. 'Sit down Roberto. Sit down with us. Have some rum. Have some pisco. Have some more Roberto. This is the best pisco in Peru. I make sure Ramon always has a few bottles here. It's my treat Roberto. I'm proud to treat you with the best pisco in Peru. Drink Roberto.' It seemed like the mayor was always there on the terrace waiting to snare him whenever he passed through. The terrace sat along one side of the town square where all the transiting trucks disgorged their loads and passengers so it required preplanning and commando action in order to escape through the few side alleys. But this time as usual he was unprepared, so, giving in to his fate, Slim just groaned and joined the crew at their table.

On one occasion prior to this, he had been so disgusted that he announced he needed to piss, walked around the back of the building and never came back. One of the mayor's cronies on these all-day drinking sessions was the chief of police. The police at that time in Peru were actually army personnel and those assigned to the highlands universally hated it. Whether it was conscious policy or not Slim didn't know but the army types in the highlands were all 'costeños' – men from the coast. They hated the cold; they hated the society; and above all, they hated the 'Indios'. On that occasion, while Slim was sitting there with the mayor, the policía sargento and some other hangers-on, an old man hobbled by wearing the home-spun clothes of the Quechua Indians – his poncho, his wool pants ending calf-high, and his ancient thin sandals. The policía sargento started yelling at him something incoherent about paying taxes then jumped up and began beating the man about his shins with his baton until he coughed up a few small coins from his pouch which the sargento then used to buy some more booze.

The mayor neither intervened nor complained that time, so this time Slim wasn't particularly thrilled by the prospect of cooling the afternoon fanning off the hot air coming out of this bad bunch.

However, today something else was going on. There was a jeep wagon parked in front, the mayor was excited and accompanied by a man Slim didn't know, presumably the owner of the jeep. The man was hulking in a shambling way with a face like an old hound dog, all creased and crevassed, with elephant ears and a large, meaty, drooping nose marked with broken veins and visible blackheads. He was introduced as the Yugoslav and the mayor wasted no more time. Vamos Roberto. We're going to the jungle. Wait a minute. What for? To catch butterflies. Butterflies? Slim didn't know anything about the weather-stained Yugoslav but the mayor didn't strike him as a butterfly type of guy. What the hell, he started to say but the mayor pushed him toward the jeep. Roberto, stop being such a pendejo. Get in. I'll tell you everything on the road. Slim wasn't exactly powerless to resist such relentless good-old-boy pressure but this sounded like a possible adventure, and when they loaded the case of rum last minute he had an inkling as to what kind of adventure it would turn out to be.

Blue Morphos. You know them? I've seen photos. Yes, yes. Big, beautiful Blue Morphos. In the jungle they are everywhere. Many, many, dozens, hundreds. We will catch them and sell them. They are very valuable. Slim became excited about the thought of seeing the fabulous Blue Morpho but dubious about catching them by the dozens for profit. He was unable to conjure a clear picture of the hulking Yugoslav flitting through the forest netting one butterfly after another or the mayor of Macusani for that matter. And would they keep them alive or sell them dead and pinned? And who would buy them and for what purpose? Questions, questions to be accompanied by answers sooner or later, but so as not to continue being the mayor's number one pendejo Slim figured to adopt a wait-and-see policy toward the whole proceeding.

A couple of hours coming down off the Altiplano following the white-water streams destined to join the Amazon and they were shacked up in a one-room cabin surrounded by banana trees and bougainvillea. Soon the first bottle of rum was ¾ gone and the Yugoslav started to talk. Slim was a fresh audience. Here was an opportunity to tell his stories again. He was a young man, having just reached fighting age, when the second world war exploded his life. Things got particularly vicious in the lands that were to become part of the republic of Yugoslavia - Serbia, Croatia, Slovenia and Bosnia. The Nazis came in so some men chose to join the fascist cause and others the communist. There arose a civil war inside the greater World War and it was ruthless and bloody. The Yugoslav was with the Chetniks – fascists – and his bunch was caught out by Marshall Tito's forces and obliterated. They were machine gunned until they lay in piles on top of each other and the Yugoslav lay underneath one particular pile pretending to be dead. He said he lay there for 12 hours underneath his dead comrades covered with their blood and shit before he was able to crawl out and escape. Marshall Tito and the communist Partisans won their war so the Yugoslav split for South America. He was wily and courageous and he worked and bluffed his way until 25 years later here he was getting old living in high country Peru telling these stories that he couldn't forget. What does he do now? asked Slim. He makes sausage, interrupted the mayor. He makes the most gawd-awful, nasty, fart-producing, belly-cramping chorizo in the whole country. And this rum is making me hungry. Come on you horse killer of a Yugoslav, let's have some lunch. As the Slav pulled a string of fat sausages out of a box and tossed them into a black encrusted skillet, Slim asked, horse killer? Sure, these sausages are horse meat. The Yugoslav explained that he cruised the countyside buying up unwanted horses, mules and donkeys. Most were old, some crippled and lame and some were dead. So, he was also a knacker man. Slim was certain this guy wouldn't be held back by the broad line definition between already dead and recently slaughtered.

The first bottle was thrown out the window and the second half gone as they started in on the frazzled sausages. It turned out the whole box was full of sausages and they were the only item on the menu for the entire two days of the great butterfly caper. No bread, no fruit, not even a banana was ripe to be eaten. As the hours plodded by and the empties crashed outside the window and the sausages went down, just as predicted the farts came on. Terrible farts combining with the effluvia of the sizzled horsemuledonkey sausages permeated and poisoned the bare-bones cabin. As the mayor of Macusani got drunker he launched into hyper-macho monologues. Yo soy el más macho de todos. I am the most. No one is more macho. When I fuck my woman for kids they are all boys. I fuck for only boys. El más. Just boys. My brother and I used to hold contests to see who was the most macho. We stood at 20 paces, each with a revolver and took turns firing closer and closer to each other's feet. Who would chicken out first? I said to my brother, Shoot me, go ahead, shoot me. I am the bravest. He put a bullet in my left calf and then ran off terrified. Look, Roberto, look. Here is the scar. I didn't cry. I didn't moan. I didn't hate my brother. Nobody is so brave. And Slim said, Nobody could be so brave. I hear you. You're the most macho of all.

As time began to blur and distort into a melange of rum and sausage and atrocious fartings, at some point a campesino named Hector came to check in with the mayor. He was accompanied by his son. Perhaps seven or eight, he was a beautiful boy with fine features and large brown eyes and the mayor demanded he sing for them. The boy demurred. He was shy but the mayor pestered Hector to have the boy sing. He had a high, soft voice and sang two narrative odes to loss and redemption that he knew by heart, and the mayor, deep in his cups, began to silently weep. At the end he threw the boy some coins on the floor.

Roberto! The mayor had finally noticed. Roberto, que te pasa? Chupa! Chupa como los buenos, no como los maricones de mierda. It had finally registered that Slim was actually not drinking as the bottles emptied and flew out the window. Slim was using the old trick of fake swallowing and fake pouring and nursing the same half glass for hours, and now the mayor of Macusani erupted in righteous indignation. Chupa Roberto! Drink! Drink like the good ones, not like the shitfull faggots. No seas maricón Roberto. Don't be a faggot. Drink like los buenos, not like those shit-eating maricones. The Yugoslav looked on silent and stolid like a sphinx with the face of a bloodhound. Slim stated how he wasn't going to drink any more rum and explained how he didn't enjoy being shitfaced and as bad as those sausages were he wasn't looking forward to vomiting them out the back door. The mayor didn't like the explanation and revved up his belligerent maricón routine even further. But Slim wasn't to be budged and, while the mayor fussed and fumed, the cadaverous Slavic Sphinx had the final say. Young Slim here has drawn his line in the sand. He will not cross no matter how hard you push him. He is strong-willed. He is the most macho. The mayor huffed and puffed some more but he slowly deflated releasing hot air until he fell silent and poured himself another glass of rum.

Slim wasn't interested in being measured on the macho scale. Right then he was investing all his energy into digesting the donkey sausage but it occurred to him as if in a dream how to reset the tone of the campaign. "How about we head out and catch us some butterflies?" Both weary sausage laden drunkards slowly swiveled their heads in his direction and stared like large, sated lizards. Roberto, are you crazy? Estás loco? You expect us to go running through the jungle chasing some fucking mariposas? We don't do that. Hector gets the butterflies for us. He'll be here soon.

But they left the cabin and the broken bottles and the

greasy skillet and, without ever seeing Hector again, headed back up the mountain slope to the top of the world. Not one Blue Morpho, not a single butterfly did he see. Of the many, the dozens, the hundreds promised, not even one to be seen. Later Slim would cut out a magnificent photo to look at occasionally and think of replacing the common metaphor of chasing wild geese with going on a wild butterfly chase.

One positive result of the caper was that from then on when passing through Macusani Slim could resist the blandishments of the mayor just by saying, "Hey, it's the lord of the butterflies."

14

THE LABORS OF HERCULES

While living among the Quechua in southern Peru Slim had secured an understanding with one of them to stay in an unoccupied hut located on the walking trail leading from the town in the valley below to the high puna beyond where they kept their herds of llamas and alpacas. The town was at 9,000 feet on the Amazon side of the spine of the Andes and his hut was 500 feet above the town. One might walk out over the top, cross mountain and gorge and eventually reach the fabled city of Cuzco but otherwise, to get anywhere you must first hike the trail down to town where a through road would take you either in one direction to the jungle or in the other to Lake Titicaca. So it was that Slim was often in town either coming or going, and sooner or later someone said, "Don't you know the mayor? She's a gringo like you." She? A gringo?

It turned out she was Swiss, a trained nurse who had come to town as part of a non-profit world health organization, had been there for years and some time ago had been elected mayor. She spoke some English but they were better off in Spanish as she hadn't been out of country for years. It was interesting to Slim what a psychological rest or relief it was to converse freely on the basis of a common western educated background. He hadn't realized how difficult it would be to communicate even the most basic themes or needs with the Quechua. Be that as it may, he stopped in to chat now and again and she always offered him a cup of coffee. The first time he disliked the flavor but out of politeness didn't say anything. However after a few coffee visits, he said "What's the matter with this stuff?" What do you mean? It just doesn't taste right. I've been drinking it for years and it tastes fine to me. Well O.K. Thanks for the cup ma'am but I'm going to investigate this if you don't mind.

Now Old Slimshanks wasn't an addicted coffee drinker and wasn't keeping any to brew in his cabin but he did enjoy a cup now and again when the opportunity presented. No sugar, no cream or milk, he liked it black but not too black. A medium roast fresh ground suited him just fine. Espresso was usually a bit too much for his liking but when he zeroed in on a big gleaming machine hissing and pulsating against the wall in a shop in Puno he was somewhat surprised but immediately ordered up a cup. He was surprised only because he had been out of 'civilization' for such a while that his mindset had twisted itself into thinking such a thing as an espresso machine couldn't exist in Peru. But Puno is a city at 12,500 feet located right on the shore of Lake Titicaca and right on the tourist route from Cuzco so it is regularly visited by many international espresso drinkers. Puno is also a market town for the Indians so it's a popular place and there are several ways to get there if you are a tourist recently arrived in Lima. One way is to ride the train steep up the mountain to Huancayo and then take the high road through Cuzco to Titicaca and on to Bolivia and La Paz if that's where you're headed.

When Slim found himself on that train elevating rapidly out of Lima he was seated opposite a garrulous Englishman who started talking and kept talking about his worldwide exploits. As he tuned him out, Slim noticed there appeared Indian boys dressed as porters walking the aisle carrying rubber bladders the size of basketballs. Rubber bladders with a crimped tube attached which the boys unfolded, held under a passenger's nose and squeezed. Oxygen! As he realized what was what with these rubber balls, he also realized there was no more braggadocio coming from the Englishman. Changing focus, Slim checked him out to see that he was slumped over in his seat seemingly passed out. The man was unconscious from oxygen deprivation. Slim decided best to leave him be and he woke up 15 minutes later after they had gone over the hump on what he soon found out was the highest train passage in the entire world.

However, that was then and Slim had been in Puno several times since without noticing the espresso machine. So it was a dramatic moment when he lifted that first cup to his lips and tasted ... what? The same damn thing. The same 'what is wrong with this coffee?' taste. It wasn't terrible, horrible, excruciatingly bad coffee. It was reasonable, drinkable but there was just something undefinably wrong. He inquired, "Where do you get this coffee?" From Juliaca, which was the same place the Swiss nurse/doctor/mayor gets hers. What do they do there? They roast it over fire in big bins. They throw in sugar and stir it around until they get to different color beans. Sugar? They roast the beans with sugar? Could this be the clue Slim had been searching for? He decided on an experiment.

Juliaca is another high altitude town on the Cuzco to Puno road and was accessible directly by truck from Slim's 'home' base, as well as from the territory beyond down the mountain side all the way into Amazonia. There were trucks passing through all the time heading for Juliaca and, though Slim had never thought to notice, some of them must be carrying coffee beans in burlap bags. Coffee likes to grow at mid-altitudes in the tropics. That would be Arabica. Robusta will thrive in the hot lowlands which is why most of what comes out of Brazil is of that variety. Mid-altitude in Peru would be from 5,000 to 7,000 feet more or less. So there would be coffee plantations below Slim's home town harvesting beans due in Juliaca for processing. Slim figured it was now time to wander around in Juliaca. It didn't take long to find the cargo zone where the trucks offloaded and lo and behold there were burlap bags of coffee piled up all over the place. There were also coffee beans strewn over the ground from split and tortured bags. These were of course green beans headed for the roaster and the sugar so Slim thought this was perfect and asked a manager type if he could help himself to some of these strewn beans.

Back home in his hut alongside the high trail, he considered the next step. How to roast his green beans was the question. He had been cooking some while staying there using a pressure cooker and a kerosene fueled primus stove. It was a continuous meal in that as the level went down in the cooker he kept adding more and reheating. Mostly cabbage leaves off of a cabbage 'tree', perennial and eight feet tall growing in front of the hut, and potatoes and freeze dried llama fat which he could purchase in flat sheets for pennies in the markets. However, there was a stove in the hut which would be much more conducive to his coffee roasting program if he could possibly fire it up. The stove was fashioned from adobe and measured about three feet long, sixteen inches wide and sat about a foot off the dirt floor. In the top were two circular holes, one eight inches wide and the other twelve. In the front was a loading 'door', the door being a flat stone to prop up or take away as you pleased. In the back was some sort of chimney thing that barely extended above the top surface of the construction.

He knew these cooking holes were formed to accommodate flat bowls manufactured to those sizes. He'd seen these bowls piled for sale in the markets, so back to Juliaca he'd have to go to purchase a couple. It was an all-day affair to get there and back or sometimes a day and a half so he waited until he had some other reason to travel out. The potters' stalls in the Andean markets are usually cluttered with dozens if not hundreds of stacked bowls. These bowls have slightly rounded bottoms and a curled two-inch lip around the edge. They are low-temp-fired and unglazed so consequently fragile and cheaply replaced. Slim purchased four of them and was pleased to see that they fit snug in the holes of his stovetop.

O.K. We've got the beans and we've got the roasting pans. Now we need some fire. Not so straightforward. There is very little wood at these altitudes so a stove like this one is designed to burn dung. That would be llama and alpaca dung. Their excrement comes in the form of round pellets similar to goats and sheep. The pellets are relatively dry and can be corralled and collected with rake or hoe. However, most of the animals there are free ranged and you are not about to wander the grasslands picking up one pellet at a time, so Slim had to find someone who often kept his llamas penned. After getting his vocabulary together – 'aka llamamanta' – begging for llama shit, he found a guy who said (probably), 'Sure, go ahead.' There were no rakes or hoes so he used a machete to scrape up a bagful and headed back to his stove.

'To Build A Fire': I could try to match Jack London and build an entire story here but let's just say it was difficult, smoky and tedious, however, build it he did and, once the dung settled in to actually burn, it burned with a glow and it burned hot enough so Slim could begin to smell the delicious aroma of roasting coffee. He kept at it for several hours stirring and shifting until all the beans looked dark brown. Now what? How much longer till that first hot cup? How to grind the roasted beans? That was the next and perhaps final question.

In front of the hut was a stone sink into which the water channeling down the mountainside along the trail could be diverted and beside that was a large flat stone with a rocker of a boulder on top. Slim knew about 'mano and metate' methods for grinding corn in Mesoamerica but this was something else. This was clearly a setup for grinding something, probably quinoa he thought, but he had never seen anything like it. It was an extremely heavy stone about 20 inches long that was flat across the top and rounded like a half-moon on the bottom. Slim poured the roasted beans onto the flat and started rocking the grinder across them. Back and forth, crunching the beans, maneuvering the rocker until there was nothing left but powder. What a beautiful thing thought Slim. Simple and beautiful.

The moment of truth is upon us. The tension is high. What will it taste like? He dumped a spoonful in his tin cup, poured boiling water on top, let it sit for a minute or two then poured the mix through his Tshirt, that being the only filter material he had available. So as not to keep you, the reader, on the edge of your chair any longer, let's cut to the chase and say, "Eureka!" Yes indeed, it was the most splendid cup of coffee he had ever tasted. Tasted just like the real thing only better. Must have been roasted sugar was the problem after all.

The next day Old Slimshanks took a sizable quota down the mountain to the Swiss lady mayornursedoctor and sat down with her to enjoy the result. Hmm, she said, that is pretty good, but looking at the meager packet she then said, "Is that all?".... IS THAT ALL? After outdoing Hercules himself. After enduring all those labors. After moving mountains and draining oceans and having the very condors dining on his liver, she says, "Is that all?"

{ 15 }

DO YOU SPEAK THIS LANGUAGE

The people of the Andes from Ecuador to Chile are spinners and weavers and knitters and plaiters and braiders. They work with fiber constantly. They harvest the wool from llamas, alpacas, vicunas, sheep, and the hair from horse tails and manes. In the country both men and women carry dropspindles and as they walk the mountain trails, they spin; as they sit watching their flocks, they spin; as they sit on their stoops in the evening, they spin. They can spin while talking, spin while walking and spin without thinking. The drive is to continuously accumulate more yarn. There is always need for more yarn. Those who make for their own, knit hats and weave belts, bags, ponchos and pants. They braid ropes out of llama wool or for more strength, out of horse hair. Those who make for sale, knit mittens, hats, socks and sweaters. Men do most of the weaving including the fabric to make the multitude of sacks used to transport potatoes, but the knitted items are done by women who set up in rows of stalls in every town to sell their wares. Old Slimshanks was forever wandering these stalls looking for another pair of socks. The socks to be purchased from these women were knitted from sheep or alpaca and were thick and warm. However, once placed inside boots and worn for two weeks they were finished, worn through and shredded at the heel, so Slim's attitude toward these home-made socks had progressed from joy and enthusiasm at first sight to pragmatically searching for the next pair.

While prowling the ubiquitous hand-made stalls Slim was exposed to the scrutiny and commentary of the ladies of the market place. These were self-sufficient women of industry and commerce. They spoke Quechua among themselves and wore home-made clothes – skirts on top of skirts, often five or six at the same time. They would pull off the bottom one when soiled and replace it with another on top. An indelible image Slim carried of these women was seeing them pissing by squatting somewhere off to the side so that the skirts hugged the ground allowing just a trickle to appear downstream. Once upon a bus ride Slim took a seat next to a Quechua woman such as these. She was carrying a baby on her lap and no sooner had Slim sat down than she pulled out a swollen breast and squirted a stream of milk just under his nose out onto the center aisle before giving it to her baby. Whooee, thought Slim. Was that just a shot across my bow, a message of abundance and fertility and an advertisement for racial and cultural pride? Or are these women just examples of raw uninhibited female power?

These formidable and earthy women were a challenge to Slim. He knew they were discussing his characteristics. From the way they laughed – one would make a comment and the others would crack-up hilarious – he imagined them saying: Look how skinny that white man is. I don't think he'd be good for anything. Or: Do you think these white boys know anything about women? But since he couldn't understand a word they were saying, perhaps they were only laughing at his silly hat. Slim really wanted to listen in and jump into the middle of their conversations and surprise them beyond measure. He was used to being surprising during his travels in Latin America. His appearance was so much of a Yankee that people automatically assumed he didn't speak or understand Spanish. But his Spanish, though not fluent, was pretty smooth and he could surprise if he chose or better yet, ingratiate with people who would otherwise be out of reach. So when he got into the Quechua speaking highlands for the first time he felt stranded. He wanted to know what these sock and sweater women were saying. Better still, he wanted to really crack them up with some sexy zinger, like, "it must be a treasure you're hiding underneath all those skirts." And not only these women, but, as Slim discovered, there are millions of Quechua speakers residing along the length of the Andes and many of them do not even speak Spanish. It would be similar to but not really the equivalent of a Navajo in the U.S. not speaking English because the Quechua have the numbers and density to carry them along in their own nation within a nation without having to engage the Spanish speakers.

Slim was chastened and irritated by these market women to the extent of wondering if he couldn't learn the language. How difficult could it be? Slim was to find out the answer to this question in short order. Impossible is not one of those adjectives that comes into play very often and it doesn't fit here either, but the word conveys the feeling of desperation that overtook Slim during his pursuit of some minimal level of comprehension. Quechua is an indigenous American language, a legacy of the Incan empire, spoken today by several million people in the areas that were part of that empire. Its construction is nothing like English or the Romance languages. Basic sentences are of course composed of subject, verb and object but not necessarily in that order which means you have to listen carefully for the grammatical signifiers and then rearrange the words in your head to come up with the meaning meanwhile losing track as the talker moves along to the next sentence and the next. The word for 'house' in Quechua is 'wasi'. If the house is the subject of your sentence it becomes 'wasiqa'. If it is the object it's 'wasita'. If you are going to the house it's 'wasiman'. If you are coming from the house it's 'wasimanta'. If you're at the house it's 'wasipi', etc., etc. That 'wasi' may be placed anywhere in the sentence and you'll only know what's going on with the house by the specific ending. The same thing happens with the verbs. Endings signifying tense or reflexives or plurals or negatives, etc., are piled on until words often become terrifyingly long and only decipherable if you can somehow get them written down and break them apart into their constituent parts.

Slim set up in a Quechua community in Peru for six months in a vain attempt to master the language, but he was privy to a vernacular masterpiece which we will reproduce here so you can savor the wonder of it. It was an insult said by his friend about another man they had just passed on a mountain trail. Slim asked: What did you just say? He repeated it and laughed. Slim pulled out a pen and notepad. Tell me again. Two words. Again. Two more words. One more time. I'll read it back to you. Is that right? Here is the insult in its entirety.

Alko akamanta motipayllakuq makta.

Let's parse it. Alko means dog. Aka = shit. Manta = out of or from. Moti = corn. Paylla is the verb, here meaning to gather or collect. Ku = reflexive. q is a nominative. Makta = man.

O.K. Now let's put it together.

Dog / shit out of / corn gather to yourself / man

Right. So even now, can you fathom what he's actually saying? The translation is: He's the kind of guy who picks corn out of dogshit. In other words: He's as low as you can go. Dogs in the Quechua highlands are not pets. They are usually skinny, cunning and desperate. They scrounge their food, and any corn in their shit might have already been twice digested from having been acquired by eating people shit, which the dogs do all the time. So, if he is the guy picking out that husk of a kernel, he's as low as one can be. Hearing this sentence going by at talking speed, you might pick up man, dog and shit if you're lucky and still be left with no idea. 'Makta' happens to be the subject of the sentence even though it arrives at the very end but in this instance, he has left off the subject signifier (maktaqa) so you don't even get that clue.

That's enough grammar for the time being or perhaps for all time. It's here not just for your amusement but also to garner some sympathy for Old Slim. He was sure there existed other people with brain architecture unlike his who could pick up on this language and be telling stories overnight but, much to his disappointment, he was never able to go back to those market ladies and shock or surprise them with a few well-placed Quechua zingers.

However he did learn enough to get by and get into trouble. He rented a hut in the southern highlands of Peru. It was situated in a hamlet comprised of a single row of buildings set along a steep path that connected the town in the valley below to more remote hamlets and estancias at the higher altitudes. Between the houses and the path ran a stoned-in aqueduct only 10" wide which brought water to all for drinking, washing and irrigating. The water could be accessed by removing a slab and allowing it to flow into a stone sink or out onto agricultural terraces cut into the hillside. Slim decided to cultivate a little plot behind the hut and plant some carrots. He figured he'd be around long enough to enjoy perhaps some baby carrots but came back from a time away to find that someone had pulled the plug at the channel and the rushing water had washed away his carrot seedlings. Slim was upset. He thought the culprits were those pesky boys living uphill and decided to make a fuss, so he stood in the doorway of their humble abode and ranted and blathered all he could think of. To judge by the looks of utter amazement on the faces of the entire family, whatever it was he actually said was probably going to be acted out and repeated for the equal amazement and amusement of many generations of unborn Indians. One could imagine some five year old down the line asking his grandfather to tell him again what the crazy white man said.

The hamlet was situated at 9,000 feet on the eastern or wet side of the Andes. That altitude at that latitude more or less demarks the upper limit of corn cultivation. There was corn in small plots alongside the path below and next to the town in the valley but only potatoes grew around the hamlet and uphill to around 11,000 feet where there was frost every night so was suitable only for llama and alpaca pasture. The farming population of the town was continually hiking back and forth in front of Slim's rented digs. They might have corn plots below, potatoes in several spots half-way up and llamas on the ichu grass up on top. The road passing through the town below came down from the Altiplano and continued on down to the jungle so that some of these farmers also cleared spots in the lowlands to grow such tropical items as bananas, cassava and avocados.

The traffic on the path in front of Slim was never empty-handed. Going up they carried empty bags and cultivating or harvesting tools and coming down were generally loaded with potatoes on their shoulders or more usually with tumplines on their foreheads. Both men and women used tumplines and often carried massive loads on their backs of branchy firewood or bundled raw wool. Most of their hand-made clay stoves were fired with dried llama dung but whatever wood they could scrounge was highly prized. Sometimes troops of llamas herded by boys with slings would go by in single file, each carrying two of those woven-from-wool 20 kilo potato sacks.

Slim had various interactions with these passers-by. He was considered an introduced exotic and they usually slowed and stared to see what strange thing he might be up to or they would whoop and holler as they passed or they might invite him to accompany them as one group did. Come with us, he thought they said, we're going hunting. One carried a shotgun and they walked far up into the hinterland where they located a small herd of cows and proceeded to shoot a young bull. Well, maybe they didn't exactly say 'hunting'. They cut him up on the spot, wrapped him in his skin and parceled out the load for the downward trek. Slim was promised, he thought, meat in exchange for carrying the bull's head for them. Upon arrival at his hut he was handed something which upon inspection turned out to be one lung. Well, maybe what he was actually promised was one lung. What was the word for lung anyway?

Another day, after he had been there for a goodly while, he was climbing the path and encountered a woman coming down overloaded with her tump-line holding a pile of twigs and branches. Carrying a load with a tump-line causes back to be bowed and head lowered allowing one to look forward with difficulty and only by peering through your eyebrows. As they approached each other, Slim thought to say a pleasant something to her because he had previously noticed women seemingly nervous when encountering him alone on the trail. He had once walked alone into one lonely village far away from any road which appeared to be curiously short of any men and as he approached, the women ran to scoop up their children and disappeared behind closed doors. Not a soul in sight and hardly a sound as he walked through. So Slim thought to assuage her fears and ask her if she'd been hilling potatoes since that's what people had been doing recently. "Hispasankichu?" he said to her. She gave him a quick, startled look of panic beneath her tump-line, scurried by and scuttled down the trail. Well, that didn't go too great. Wait a minute. What did I say to her? Let's see . . . the 'chu' at the end makes it a question so that was okay and the verb for the hilling of potatoes is 'haspiy' but wait a minute... I said 'hispay'. What does that mean? Oh damn! That is the verb 'to piss'. I just asked her if she had been pissing!

There is a character in Quechua folklore called the ñak'aq. The ñak'aq is to be encountered along lonely trails well away from the villages in the mountains. He is to be greatly feared because he traps Indians to harvest their fat. He wants only Indian fat, it was explained to Slim, because Misti fat is loose and watery and Indian fat is solid and best for making candles. The ñak'aq is said to be tall with ghastly white skin and hair on his face. He strides the mountain trails wearing a black cloak and a black hat and harvests Indian fat for making candles. This phantasm strikes terror into the hearts of especially women and children, they being the more vulnerable. Slim pondered this character after the incident with the woman on the trail. He thought about his resemblance to a possible ñak'aq. That would help explain the reactions of native women in the mountains to his appearance, however, ñak'aq or no, asking a woman if she had just been pissing is asking to be treated as if he were one. He thought about the women in the market place. They would just laugh at what he had said. They feared no ñak'aq. But the more Slim thought about it, the more he figured it was time to punt. He wasn't going to gain the whole ten yards. He had bought his last pair of socks and said his last Scrabble word in this impossible language. He was going to sell his pressure cooker to the Maryknoll priest in town and get together 15 varieties of potatoes, all colors, shapes and sizes to take with him, and head on home.

THEY DO THINGS IN BRAZIL

If you ever think to consider Bolivia, the images in your mind are probably of llamas and alpacas and Quechua and Aymara indians wearing ponchos and knitted hats with ear flaps. Or women with layers of voluminous skirts and bowler hats. Or snowy peaks of the high Andes in the midst of which runs the endless dry, cold Altiplano. Or Lake Titicaca, the highest large lake in the world. Or La Paz, at 12,000 feet the highest capital city in the world. What you probably don't conjure about Bolivia is that within its political boundaries lies more tropical and subtropical land than mountains and Altiplano. These hot, wet lowlands descend to the east from the Andes out toward Amazonia and toward Brazil, and, as Slimshanks contemplated crossing the 400 miles from the last Bolivian outpost at the base of the foothills to the Brazilian border, he decided to take the train.

Old Slim had been traveling the Andean highlands for months wending his way in no hurry southward and had accommodated to dry and cool and intense sunny days and frigid nights, so the fetid, rancid and fly blown city of Santa

Cruz, full of horses and burros and migrants on the make, didn't really strike him just then as charming or picturesque. And the thought of procuring rides through more, or actually less, of the same for 400 miles sent him to the train station. It seemed semi-miraculous to Slim that Bolivia had thought to and managed to build a track here at all. But it was flat land from Santa Cruz on east and Brazil after all was the regional economic powerhouse so one could understand the motivation behind the project.

He wasn't unhappy to be leaving Bolivia. Throughout its post-colonial history Bolivia had changed governments on an average it seemed of every few months. The man in power at the moment was another shithead of a general who was backed by the U.S. because the last guy he knocked out was certainly a 'leftist'. There were full sized portraits of himself decked out in every medal it might be possible to accumulate in a military lifetime and signs saying things like "Bolivia, ámela o déjela." Doesn't that sound quite familiar? However, the generals and other government thieves are one thing and the current of everyday life is another and Slim found himself enjoying life on the streets of La Paz. The city tumbles down off the level plain into a massive ravine so that the narrow, meandering streets are sometimes almost vertical and they presented a continual moveable feast. There were sidewalk vendors selling everything from skewered chunks of lamb to dark, malty beer whipped up with eggs in a blender. He ate all his meals on the sidewalks sampling all the availabilities while wondering occasionally where this stuff had been before he put it in his mouth. Often when turning just the right corner he would be awestruck once again by the massive snowy bulk of Illimani, all 20,000 feet of it in the extraordinary clarity of light shining in the thin air above the city.

When he asked for the cheapest tickets for the train ride to Brazil, the clerk looked at him strangely and he wondered why until he boarded as directed into the last two cars which were filled with Indian campesinos and all their bundles and babies. There were long rows of wooden benches situated along the walls all occupied and plenty of floor space filled with bodies and bundles so Slim took it upon himself to walk upstream through the cars until he arrived at one that seemed a reasonable facsimile of what you might expect for railroad travel and took a seat next to a window. When the conductor, working his way along checking tickets, arrived at Slim he informed him this was first class and Slim belonged back with the lower class. Now Slim was conscious of the favoritism you might wrangle in certain situations just by acting like an American who believed himself master of the universe. He had occasionally acted the part, for example walking right by a doorman into an exclusive hotel where he had no right to be, but that was not typically his way and he prided himself on his ability to commune with the locals and mix and mingle in any situation. However, this time he really just didn't feel like moving out of that seat and didn't want to cough up any more money so he slid into playing dumb. You have to move back. Yes, yes, this is a good seat. You have the wrong ticket. Yes, yes, very good. Everything is very good. You must go back and buy another ticket. That's good. Very good. Thank you for asking. The conductor gave up in exasperation and turned to the paying audience and said, "Este Gringo no sabe nada. Es un idiota."

The culture shock at the Brazilian border was dramatic. On the Bolivian side were burros, carts, dusty Indians and directly across the Brazilian line was a bus stop with a glassed-in enclosure to which a gleaming new bus came, opened its doors with a pneumatic sigh and spilled into the day's heat a couple of riders and a rush of air-conditioned cool. That an invisible line on the earth could signify so much, thought Slim, as all of a sudden he could understand nothing of what anybody was saying. Portuguese! The Brazilians were disdainful and even if they could, refused to speak Spanish. However, Slim quickly procured a ride out of town. It was a long distance diesel hauling a trailer piled high with plastic sewer pipe. They were headed to São Paulo close to 1,000 miles to the east and the driver pointed to the trailer saying sure, ride on the pipe if you want. Sailing on coconuts was one thing but riding for hundreds of miles on a pile of plastic pipes just about boggled Slim to the limit. The road was none too smooth as he battered and bounced along this route that cut through the southern edge of the Mato Grosso and for hours on end there was no sign of civilized life. They passed through vast marshy savannas like the Everglades filled with wading birds, interspersed with deep forest and grassy open spaces. There was no agriculture and no people. Every twenty five miles or so there appeared a roadside truck stop, every one of which the driver idled into, thank God said Slim, in order to throw down a tiny espresso cup of the blackest, strongest, sweetest coffee Slim had never imagined.

Brazil grows sugar, so much that they turn it into alcohol to power their automobiles, and Brazil grows coffee, not the prized Arabica but the rugged Robusta, more than any other country. So, load the cup half-full with sugar and top it off with the concentrated essence of Robusta and hand it out free to drivers and passengers all along the endless, lonely highway from the Bolivian border. Slim assumed the government was subsidizing the free café program to keep drivers so jittery they would be insensible to the lulling mezmerizing of the highway sirens. The jitters wouldn't help Slim absorb the punishment of the pipes but he was grateful for the pit stops and thought he should have brought along a bag of coca leaves from Bolivia. He was thinking that the phlegmatic and tireless Indians of the high Andes would be chewing coca and riding these pipes without the slightest protest.,By the time the road from Bolivia crosses the mighty Paraná River, the land has trnsformed into lush green farm and ranch country. This is the prosperous heart of rural Brazil. The Paraná is wide and carries an immense amount of water. Slim knew from the maps that it still had 1,000 miles to go before reaching Buenos Aires and the South Atlantic and 300 miles before crashing over the massive falls of Iguaçu.

After crossing the Paraná, the pipe truckers pulled over for a nap at a town called Presidente Prudente where Slim bid them Godspeed and ambled into a town that was eerily deserted. Where is everybody, he asked a storekeep who was the only one still manning his shop. At the feria, he said, pointing that way. It happened to be that time of year – time for the annual agricultural fair and the entire town was out there at the rural edge living it up. Cows and horses and sheep and a Ferris wheel and rodeo and barbecues and cotton candy and horse racing and arcade games and beer parlors – it was all happening as Slim walked into the crowd. He was just beginning to get oriented when a girl walked up to him and started talking. She appeared to be about 18, had seen him as a stranger and began in English. That emerged unintelligible so he suggested Spanish. That worked better and wouldn't he like to come to her house which was close to the fair grounds and have a nice meal? Surely he would after eating nothing but road food for the last forever. She was accompanied by two friends – an attractive blond and a boy who seemed somewhat younger than the two girls. Slim followed them through the front door and right into her bedroom where she immediately asked didn't he want to fuck her? Somewhat dumbfounded, he hummed and hawed while she lay down on her back, put her hand down her jeans and started wriggling and moaning. She was short and plump and conveyed the kind of heat that might be radiated by an oversexed chipmunk, while the blond lay next to her with a bemused look, not really participating, and the boy came close to him to whisper, when you're through with her how about me too? Slim stared at him and not really abashed, he said, "This is Brazil. We do things here." Slim thought people do things everywhere but how about lunch? With great sadness he realized there was going to be no nice meal so he said goodbye to the friendly trio and walked out contemplating the equation between sex and lunch. $X(X^2) \neq X^3$ where X is the value of lunch and X^2 is the value of sex. The whole thing could go exponential, but if there is no lunch, the value of X is zero so not only do you not raise satisfaction to the third power, but the whole equation collapses to nothing. As he passed by the living room on his way out there was a man sitting there he assumed to be the father who rolled his eyes at Slim and shrugged as if he were accustomed to this play acted out by his chipmunk daughter.

Welcome to Brazil. As he wandered back onto the fair-grounds, he cogitated - were these just horny kids or was this a sneak preview into the whole country? Everybody was certainly friendly but the offer of this trio seemed above and beyond the call of duty. However that may be, he grav-itated to the rodeo corrals and climbed onto the planked fence to watch calf roping and bulldogging. There was a group of skilled cowboys who seemed to be collecting all the prizes and who were riding exceptional, highly trained quar-ter horses. As he watched, he realized that two of them were speaking English – not merely English but what sounded a lot like Texan. During a lull he cornered one of them and af-firmed that yeah they were down here from Texas for a while to check up on the ranch. They were the King Ranch, had a big spread nearby, and had brought in some cow ponies to show off their stuff at the fair. Well, well, said Slim. Wouldn't the King Ranch consider hiring a fellow American on his own in Brazil in need of a job?

Four days later, they handed him a halter, pointed him to the corral and said go get yourself a horse. Now, during the interview for this job, they had asked Slim just one question, "Can you ride a horse?" He didn't lie or make up tall tales – he just said yes. He could. He was a lily white suburban boy who had been set up with riding lessons as a nine year old. Walk, trot and post on an English saddle round and round a small paddock. Posting had always remained a problem without a solution. It always found him going up when the horse was coming down and coming down when the horse was pushing up. He never found this to be congenial, and he knew that cowboys don't post, so, sure, he could ride. But the foreman took pity on him that first morning: he plunged into the maelstrom of horses Slim had churned up and emerged with the horse to launch Slim's cowpunching career.

All the cow ponies used on the ranch were mares. This one was chubby and genial and worked as if on automatic pilot so Slim was feeling plenty confidant until the next day when he recognized that mare hitched to a buggy. They had especially given him for his first ride their old reliable buggy horse – a mount they had removed from the daily work rotation and semi-retired to trot the lightweight buggy around the ranch roads. Slim was touched. He was expecting a hazing of sorts, a probing or testing of his true grit factor – a behavior with which he was quite familiar, to be found among groups of tough men doing difficult or dangerous jobs.

Except for the buggy mare, the horses in the corral were yesterday's workers. At the end of the working day they were kept corralled until the following morning when they were released into the field with the others that were not chosen for that day's work. The process of choosing each morning Slim thought was amazing. One rider would run his yesterday's horse out and around what was referred to as 'the troop' (a tropa) and whoop and whistle them in. The troop would thunder into a dead-end corner of the pasture and, knowing the routine, would start to line up facing in against the fence from the corner out in both directions. There were possibly 40 horses, all quarter horse mares from King Ranch stock, and they aligned themselves with some rough encouragement from the boys along both wings of the fence. There were five cowboys plus Slim and as the foreman walked along the ranks designating this one and that one as today's workers, each cowboy pushed between the close-packed rumps, slipped on a halter and led his mount out to be bridled and saddled. The troop waited more or less patiently until the last one was designated and withdrawn, then began to whiffle and shuffle anticipating the foreman's whistle, and then wheeled, catapulted and exploded out of there in a delirious melee.

There is a certain amount of romance and adventure that has attached itself to the idea of the life of a cowboy. There are other professions Slim could think up in this same category: engineers on freight trains; drivers of cross-country 18 wheelers; boilers of maple syrup; perhaps even astronauts, that are perceived to be adventurous and thus romanticized but in reality are characterized by nothing so much as tedium. Long stretches of tedium punctuated by repetitive action shadowed by the remote possibility that something might cascade out of control at any minute. Sitting on a horse watching cows all day is incontestably tedious. Perhaps on an open range of sagebrush across vast acreages of wild country there would be adventure to find you but on a modern beef operation of fenced pastures and mowed fields, there are few challenges for a cowboy to tackle. The job description for Slim and the boys was simple – keep a lookout over a herd of 100 cows for any one coming into heat, cut her out of the herd, escort her to a clamping chute at the edge of the field and artificially inseminate.

The King Ranch, which at that time had merged with Swift foods to form a mega-meat empire, had come up with its own breed of beef cow. They named it the Santa Gertrudis and it looked at first glance like a Hereford, hornless and showing the same coloration, but on second look was shorter legged. plumper and dare I say, more beefy. Their body type inclines more in the direction of a pig than a cow. To continue the genetic line and insure the ever increasing beefiness of the breed, every brood cow is artificially inseminated. The bull, or bulls, of the year are carefully chosen and kept in Texas, and the semen is stored frozen and sent out to wherever there are Santa Gertrudis ready to be bred. When cows are kept in a herd it is not difficult to determine which is in heat at the moment. Looking out over the sea of identical brown bodies, it is the one with head in the air riding the back of a neighbor. It does require a cowboy's skill to run down that cow, cut her out of the herd and get her to the inseminator. The horses know the routine and love to chase cows. If you keep cows and horses in the same pasture, the horses will always dominate and sometimes will chase the cows just for fun. Without any direction from the rider, those trained cow ponies would stick on the designated cow no matter the twists and turns but the key was, as Slim discovered his first day on the artificial insemination circuit, to point the horse at the right cow to begin with. After weaving all over the lot scattering cows right and left, he looked up to see two of the boys sedately escorting the cow in question to the chute. They laughed at Slim but they were remarkably tolerant of this stranger who had come out of nowhere and was obviously a dilettante.

Besides escorting hot cows to the inseminator, there was only one other job to do at regular intervals. When the grass in one pasture was chewed down the herd was moved to the next. To accomplish this task however required hardly any input from the cowboys except for opening a large gate and whistling. The whistle alerted two large Brahma steers that were kept with the herd of beefers. They were light gray, almost white, with horns pointing straight up and humps on their backs and they always kept to themselves, grazing apart from the obtuse, little peasants. They were obviously reincarnates who tolerated their position but with disdain in their hearts. Upon seeing a cowboy go to the gate and hearing the whistle, the Brahmas walked with dignity through into the adjoining pasture and the entire herd of cloned hoi polloi rushed out after them.

However, time slowed and drowsed through the tropical afternoons, and waiting and watching for the next cow to heat up was none too exciting, and these King Ranch cowboys were basically kids. There were no Gabby Hayes type grizzled veterans in the crew. They were all in their twenties and appeared to be fun loving boys dressed in jeans and tee shirts. Some didn't even bother with hats. They devised games to pass the time. They would mark out 50 to 100 meter straight tracks and then run horse races – sometimes straight out sprints and other times relays, passing a lighted cigarette back and forth as a baton. Or they would retire to a dusty stretch under some trees along a back fence to see which could lay the longest skid mark. That involved spurring your horse to full speed from a dead stop and then reining her until her rump almost touched the ground and her front legs held stiff in front, the boys cheering and critiquing.

The boys loved their cigarettes. They each carried a pouch within which was a solid hunk of black, greasy tobacco. Every day started at 5 am and, as the mist still lay across the fields, the first place they would go after saddling up was the corn crib. The dry corn was stored ear and husk and they each ripped off a couple of husk pieces to stash in the pouch with the tobacco. As the day progressed they would shave off flakes of tobacco with their knives, cut a rectangle of husk and roll the two together to make a smoke sticking it together with a wet lick. Along with smoke they also consumed mate/ all day. Each carried one of those special mate/ gourds inlayed with silver and pierced by a silver strainer-straw. These gourds are ubiquitous among Brazilian cowboys and Argentine gauchos all the way down through Patagonia. They would fill them with yerba mate/ and hot water before they left the bunkhouse in the morning and refill at the lunch break.

Slim hadn't suffered much more than some full-body stiffness after riding the sewer pipe for a day, however even just the first day riding cowboy for 6 – 8 hours left him groping for his hammock. After several days there were open sores on his rear and thighs and he came to the conclusion God didn't intend for mankind to pass his days on top of a horse. But time heals mostly everything and he became what is known in the vernacular as 'hard assed'. The food supply was plentiful but monotonous – rice, beans, beef, coffee for every meal and in the evening he would join them to watch a daily soap opera – "Selva de Pedra" – The Stone Jungle – a drama which enraptured the boys, all about loving, living and suffering in the wicked big city.

He'd been on the ranch for some weeks and didn't mind the life but he began to ponder the way back home. Perhaps he would go up the coast from Rio, cross the mouth of the Amazon and proceed on north in the Guyanas then figure how to somehow get back to the U.S. from there. It had been a few years but he wasn't really feeling homesick just somehow a little lethargic, something he couldn't quite put his finger on. He liked getting up at dawn and riding out into the rising sun. He liked watching the boys cut out a precise rectangle of corn husk with their sheath knives and make their cigarettes. He liked working with those remarkable horses. He admired their beauty, power and athleticism. He liked the enigmatic Brahmas. But he didn't feel like whooping it up with the boys when they were passing around a bottle of white lightning, and he wondered if he weren't just getting tired of being a stranger until one day he was off his horse pissing onto the grass when he was jolted out of his reverie noticing his urine was coming out almost black. That evening he asked one of the boys to look into his eyes. What color do you see? Laranja. The following morning he didn't saddle up but went to the big house where the owner spoke English to request a ride to the nearest doctor. The receptionist said knock on the door and go in. As the door swung open, the doctor who was sitting opposite behind his desk looked up, pointed his index finger at Slim's face and said, "Hepateetees!"

{ 17 }

RIDING THE BEAST
TO MONK CITY

It all started with a knock on the door. It was in the quiet, leafy suburbs outside of New York City. Old Slimshanks had retired and repaired to the family home long vacated by siblings after escaping Brazil with a case of 'hepateetees' announced by the local doctor upon seeing his orange eyes. Slim was scrubbed and shaved and clean-clothed and luxuriating in the quiet calm of the mid-afternoon house in its cul-de-sac when he opened the door to his old friend Perk. The surprise was intense and Perkins just stood there grinning. 'What the hell...! How the hell...! Am I hallucinating?' Slim looked around in front of the house and saw no car, no taxi, no bicycle and there was Perk with his huaraches, his side bags and his pack looking hairy and leathery and self-reliant just as he had a year before in Nicaragua. Slim had a sudden sense of dislocation as if he were caught acting the role of somebody he wasn't, living a soft life in this soft house. He and Perk had spent the past few years as itinerant gringos in Latin America hanging out in mountain and jungle with indios and campesinos and wandering hippies from all over the world. They had shared some adventures, had inhaled plenty, had gone long stretches unshaven and unshorn but had lost touch an eon ago when Slim headed into South America.

And here he was now standing grinning in the doorway and God only knows how he got there or how he figured Slim would actually be present. He had figured it right though and had caught Slim just on the cusp of wanting to bust out back into the scrum of things. Perk had grown up in Iowa and wanted to catch Slim by surprise before heading back to Des Moines. It was only about 1500 miles to the monk city but, so what, Perk shrugged. You hitched ten, you hitched a thousand – he'd get there soon enough. Slim knew how it was all right but he'd rather hitch the two-lane highways in Colombia or Ecuador than the interstates in the U.S. and he started to ponder the possibilities.

Slim of course was well aware that one could not be considered a genuine citizen/resident of these United States without owning at least one automobile. So he wasn't long into his R&R before purchasing one. He found a likely suspect in the newspaper for a few minimal hundreds and brought it home to the annoyance of his mother. Within this cute little suburban circle of houses, all other vehicles were hidden away in garages so that no foreign objects broke up the clean sweep of curb and lawn except this one, which Slim had nicknamed The Beast. It was the best America had to offer in its time, discounting Cadillacs, but its time had passed twenty years prior. The car was a 1953 Chrysler New Yorker, built when Detroit was designing and manufacturing automobiles to last. It was a tank, huge and heavy and loaded with steel. And there it was sitting along the curb in front of the house with no place to go except . . . why not Des Moines? Hey! Let's fire up The Beast and head out across America like genuine 1950s Americans. We'll skip the interstates and float along on the back of the old Beast down the state highways the whole way. I don't know about the genuine Americans part, said Perk, or the floating part but otherwise it's an offer that can't be refused.

Slim had not been one of those American adolescents who spend half of their growing-up years either underneath an automobile or underneath a hood. He was a genuine automotive innocent. Put in the gas, turn the key, watch the yellow line, and proceed with the full faith and confidence of the ignorant. So it doesn't take fresh chicken entrails or an eagle flying backwards or an eclipse of the sun to augur at this point that stuff was about to happen. Like children of Eden they hopped The Beast and blasted west blowing gasoline out the tail pipe like it was water. And it was! Due to some historical anomaly or incomprehensible gas war the price at the time was 15 cents/gallon, a price the world hadn't seen since John D. formed Standard Oil. Did they bother to check the engine oil, or the radiator, or anything else? Of course not, so maybe they were lucky they didn't lose the engine or have the drive train grind itself to pieces or run all the tires flat, but very soon Perk had to switch from the role of complacent passenger to stagecoach whip.

The stuff that did happen started soon and manifested in The Beast behaving badly after a long run. He refused to start. That is, you turned the key and nothing happened, but only sometimes. And worse yet he would stall at the most inappropriate times and fall dead. The Beast was growing cranky. But Perk was up to the challenge. The solution to the problem was to get people to pushstart. If we stalled out at a red light in one of the innumerable small towns dotting the pre-interstate highways in middle America and the pileup commenced to honk madly, he would jump out, run back to the unfortunate behind them and demand he bumper up and push. The light was green, horns were howling, drivers were leaning out their windows yelling and cursing and if Perk had to use terror, he would terrorize or if he needed diplomacy, he would cajole, and with a little push The Beast would roar into life and be gone from that town.

Other occasions led to other scenarios. They would leave the engine running at gas stations, flouting the adamant signs telling the ignorant public to turn them off, or look for some kind of a slope and point The Beast downhill if they were leaving it to go in and eat somewhere. This latter tactic lost its appeal the farther west into the flatlands they went so they transformed the problem into a game. Who among the welter of people everywhere would really like to push us into life? They would sit stalled in supermarket parking lots and restaurants and gas stations and settle in to discuss and assess the pushing potential of each human to come into view. Good, possible or no way – they would get rated and then asked, pleaded or begged. The most enthusiastic pushers were groups of teenage boys hanging out together – this was a lark and good for lot of laughing. The next best was a farmer in a pickup – no problem boys, he would say, and bumper to bumper. Not all men driving pickups would qualify – Slim would look at clothes, facial expressions or what sort of stuff was in the truck bed to deliver a rating potential. Most women were automatic nos – except if she were wearing blue jeans and boots and had a smile on her face.

Things came to a head in the middle of the night in Michigan. Slim's brother James was ensconced at the time in the university in Ann Arbor so they figured to hole up with him for a day or two before trying the final leg to Des Moines. The timing worked out such that they were still bowling along after dark in an attempt to get there before lights-out when The Beast gave up for the day, sighed, hiccupped and shambled to a dead stop beside the road. Perk and Slim looked at each other, shrugged and tucked themselves in against the doors to await the dawn only to be violently awakened at some gawdawful hour when only goblins and ghouls are at loose in the world. The passenger-side door that supported Perkins' sleeping body was ripped open leading to his rude awakening in the snow and roadside gravel. The perpetrator was an officer of the law, a midnight cop cruising the district looking for trouble. "What are you guys doing here? Get this piece of shit out of here." Sorry officer. Can't get it started. If you'll be so kind as to give us a push . . . "What the hell are you talking about? If you're not gone next time I come by, you'll be in real trouble." Goblins, ghouls and cops – they shrugged again and went back to sleep.

Brothers are sometimes remarkably similar characters and sometimes they are not. Whereas Slim knew nothing about automobiles, James knew everything. On top of that he had made Ann Arbor connections who knew even more. Not only was the University of Michigan in Ann Arbor but the mighty General Motors itself had set up a college there to train automotive engineers, and James had followed his nose to make some friends among those guys. They formed a posse and came to the rescue. Embarrassingly all it took was a battery to wake up The Beast and get him parked somewhere near the dorms. Then all the motor-heads convened together underneath the hood of the patient in question and emerged with a diagnosis – the voltage regulator had ceased to function. A voltage regulator is an inscrutable item. It seemed to Slim to be somewhat of a voodoo magician. If the battery is not fully charged the regulator permits the juice generated by the generator to flow into it; contrary-wise, if the battery is charged the regulator decides to divert the flow and sends it to some unknown fate. All this happens automatically inside a little black box and how the vitals inside the box make those decisions was a complete mystery to Slim. But not however to a friendly little old man to whom the posse directed Slim with his black box. He opened the box, took a pair of pliers and bent one thin brass tang one way and another thin brass tang another way, closed the box, handed it back and said, "That should take care of it." It is something to do with electromagnetism. The mystery and magic of electricity are related to the mystery and magic of magnetism and that little old man was a wizard in disguise.

All that pleading, cajoling and terrorizing of otherwise innocent American drivers left unhinged in their wake like compasses having lost true-north – all because of an un-charged battery. It boggled the mind and Slim thought, we've been in Latin America too long. He recollected riding through the Peruvian Andes in the back of a big truck with about thirty Indians and all their worldly possessions, pounding into miles of potholes, when the driver/owner stopped and declared that a rear leaf spring was broken and he was going to fix it. He ushered everybody off the truck and proceeded to run that dual wheel up onto the biggest bolder they could roll in from beside the road and then run it off with a mighty crash. He repeated the action about ten times, the crashings sounding very satisfying and heal-ing, then ordered everybody back on and we potholed for-ward to our destination. Slim was thinking this was that sort of mindset that could have creeped into his brain just like the worm that migrates into the brain of a moose and ren-ders him like those de-magnetized compasses. However that may be, they were on the road again feeling carefree and propelled by magic. Gasoline was still 15 cents/gallon and The Beast was bawling down the highway free and easy to the monk city. Whenever you see the words 'free and easy' do you not suspect there might appear a cloud on the hori-zon? A wee cloud that just possibly might spread and darken and bode bad weather? How dark? That is the question. Well, they rolled to a halt in front of the Perkins residence in Des Moines and celebrated. They had gotten the Perk back home, but just barely. They hobbled and limped through the home stretch but by all the gods in the monastery, there they were in the monk city. However, The Beast was motionless once again - the transmission was shot.

At this point Slim could have called in the junk man to come and haul The Beast away ignominious and defeated, and hopped the Greyhound back to Yorkville. He had planned on driving back on his lonesome but the chances of finding another transmission for a '53 Chrysler New Yorker were next to none and trying to fix this one seemed an exercise in futility. But he tried anyway – probably that brain worm on the move again. He had the thing apart on the Perkins cellar floor in a thousand pieces – roller bearings by the hundreds scattered everywhere – when Perk suggested they go see Dangerous Dan. Dangerous (El Peligroso) was then set up in his home town in Minnesota just to the north of Iowa on the map. Slim hadn't seen him since he and Valda were grinding each other to pieces in their Tasbaponie hammock on the Caribbean coast of Nicaragua. Slim didn't yet know what had become of all that but he was about to find out and the Dangerous One was only a days' drive away. Roller bearings left behind on the floor, they drove deeper into the winter to find Dan in fine shape and Valda gone. The combination of cold weather and colder family had propelled her out of Minnesota back to her tropical homeland. Valda aside, the conversation soon migrated to the topic of The Mighty Beast.

"A '53 Chrysler," said Dan. Hmmm. I wonder. Is it a big car? All rounded fenders and curved top, hood and trunk? Yep, that's it. They built those early fifties cars to look just like Dwight Eisenhower. "Well, this is a long shot but there is a junker sitting in a field by the road just north of town that's been there about as long as I can remember which might just possibly be the same car." No way! We're talking a miracle here. There's only one way to find out, said Dan, and picked up the phone. This guy is going to meet us out there. He's a high school buddy of mine. Works in the local service station and he's bringing a wrecker. A wrecker! The Dangerous One, having obviously expelled his Latin brain worm, was now springing into action.

It was covered with snow and sunk to its hubs in the sod but from the road it looked possible. Perk was brushing off the snow around the back searching out those chromed letters. By God, here it is! 'New Yorker' right there on the back of the trunk. We're in miracle territory now boys. Get down on your knees and face Mecca or talk to the Buddha or pray to the Christ that the transmission is actually still there. Pray all you want said the wrecker man but get out of the way, and he pounded across the ditch, through the snow and backed the rig at 90o into the side of the junkmobile. It was mid-winter in Minnesota and that Chrysler had been sitting there subsiding for years, so when they ran the cable over the roof and attached the big hook under the rocker panel to the far side frame and the man wound up the winch - what do you think happened? The front wheels of the wrecker started to lift off the ground; the winch commenced to scream; the cable began to cut a groove into the roof; the Chrysler exploded out of the frozen earth leaving big hunks of rubber behind. It was then balanced on its passenger-side doors with the underside drive train now exposed making it a piece of cake to unbolt the transmission and ride it like the Prince of Wales back to Des Moines.

A long and tedious and uneventful drive it was for Slim back to the New York suburbs. The obverse, the back-track, the other side of the coin it was from the ride west. After swapping the trannies, replacing the petrified gunk with fresh fluid and test driving the streets of Des Moines, The Beast was once more the king of the road; the Cruise-America-Mobile; the pride of Detroit; and he ran those 1500 miles east with nary a complaint.

But Slim had other plans and other places to be and The Beast just didn't fit into his long-range so he put it up for sale and left it with brother James to negotiate. Slim was gone and James was finished with Ann Arbor and back home for a while. The price was low and the parents wanted that beasty thing out of the neighborhood so the bait was caste and the hook brought in a strange and maybe somewhat 'challenged' kid who was after his first automobile. James gave him explicit instructions on how to start it – that is 'never pump the accelerator' – and the kid called him after a couple of days. "Hey Jim. The car won't start." Well, what have you been doing. "Sure, first I pump the accelerator then...". Perhaps a week or two later James took another call from him. "Hey Jim. Did you steal the car?"

{ **18** }

THE POWER RANGER

When you are hanging out in Penn Station in New York City waiting for your scheduled Greyhound, it's the people who provide the comic and tragic relief. The vast vaulted spaces of the old railroad terminus are channeled with people. They are striding with great purpose in and out the portals, intersecting, some on diagonals, some straight across. They are standing expectant in small family groups circled like wagon trains around their luggage. They are leaning against the walls alone with a plastic bag or one suitcase, staring vacantly into the abyss of their future. They are slumped asleep in the corners. They are nervous and tired of waiting, pacing and checking the big clock on the wall. There are kids with no discernable luggage save a boom-box on their shoulder jiggling to their tunes by a departure door going maybe only to Newark or Baltimore. There are soldiers, GIs in uniform with their duffel bags. There are students headed back to school sitting bored on their stuff. There is also a lot of what might be called low-life that accumulates in a bus terminal in America. You could pick out this flotsam from among the regular surge and flow by their irregular wakes. Pickpockets, conmen, sex slaves, drunks and cruising opportunists meandered through the crowd.

Anybody with money in the U.S. doesn't ride the Greyhound. Long distance buses are usually the first resort of the carless or the shiftless or the homeless and the last resort of plain folks saving money. So what was Old Slim doing there guarding a pile of cardboard boxes waiting on the next bus to Dallas? Getting there the cheapest way possible is the answer. The boxes represented considerable wealth in the form of maple syrup jugs that he was calling luggage and thus saving a hefty shipping charge to Texas. At the same time he was killing the other bird by transporting his family to a big anniversary celebration. They were a family of four and the boxes were ten and Old Slim was going to make damn sure they stayed on a bus with them all the way. They had ridden the first leg from Vermont, the syrup being fresh made and boxed for the trip, and had escorted the maple into a pile on the floor in Penn Station when Slim settled down to survey the display of homo sapiens.

His eyes roamed as he gazed wearily and warily at the maelstrom but suddenly were stopped, riveted by a figure standing 50 feet across the hall next to a stone pillar edging one of the portals. He didn't recognize the man; he wasn't dressed out of the ordinary and he wasn't physically distinctive in any special way, but Slim's gaze was held by some sort of magnetism. The man was radiating energy. Energy and power – it was pouring out of him. Slim quickly looked around. It seemed no one else noticed but Slim fixed on him from across the room. He was maybe 35 wearing blue jeans and a T-shirt and was standing forward up on the balls of his feet with his legs apart. In a fighter's crouch but not crouching, and, whereas everyone else in sight was dozing or dreaming or doddering the time away, this guy was enveloped in mega-wattage, giving off sparks checking out everything and everybody. Slim thought – who is this guy? What were the possibilities? He is either an escaped lunatic who believes he is the second coming of Jesus and is in Penn Station in order to save these sad humans from their various fates; or he is so stoned on something he feels he has swallowed the sun; or he is Count Dracula looking for his next victim. Slim really had no idea except that the man was concentrated energy and about to blow in some direction. Why did nobody else notice? Maybe it's the country vs city thing? City people pass their days in surfeit and as a result don't bother to look at each other out on the street, whereas Slim lived with his maple trees and liked looking at faces. He even smiled at some pretty ones although this behavior seemed to bother most people. Mind your own business is the city's mantra. When Slim looked back the man was gone. Gone; leaving Slim perplexed and amused – who was that guy?

No more time to ponder. They had to get those boxes through the door onto the loading platform and into the Dallas Greyhound, and the four of them into their seats. The rest of the passengers filed on and settled in, one of them being a young black man who sat in the row right in front of Slim and Jo. Slim watched him come on and registered something amiss about the guy but what it was or might be he just shrugged off. When are we going? asked one of the kids. Soon. All the seats are full and the driver's about to fire up.

What the hell? Two men burst through the door and up the few steps at the front of the bus. The one in front stood filling the aisle studying the passengers. Holy shit! It was none other than the magnetic man! The power ranger. What was going on? Quickly Mr. Mega-Watt moved down the aisle, grabbed the kid in front of them by the scruff and slammed him onto the floor of the bus. Slim was outraged and about to jump up and protest – what the hell do you think you're doing? But in the same instant, the realization hit that this power ranger was way out of his league and up to something he knew nothing about, so shut up, sit down, and watch. They dragged the kid out of the bus and instantly had him splayed face down on the concrete platform. While Slim watched through the window, the power ranger reached into the kid's coat and pulled out a pistol. Cops. They were undercover cops. Slim had been zeroing in on the power ranger on the job. On the prowl; on the trail; sniffing and spying, his antennae supercharged – a hunter of humans. Somebody allowed by the law to do whatever dirty work; it rendered him all-powerful and he loved it.

Slim felt his heart pounding in his ears and realized he had been holding his breath for far too long. He inhaled, noticed his hands were shaking and thought to himself – I've been living in the woods now for quite a while. The driver pushed the pneumatic button that hissed the door closed and rolled the bus out of there as if nothing unusual had occurred. The busload of riders didn't seem too affected either and even though Slim craned his neck, the man hunter and his prey had disappeared.

Leaving New York City behind, leaving those juiced up cops in fantasyland, riding the big bus across America; what else could possibly happen? As Slim and family stood in the parking lot in Dallas, once again guarding their pile of maple boxes, he reflected on that question. During his travels in Latin America he had hopped the bus now and again when he felt tired of begging rides beside the road, and initially was confounded by the laxity of the timetables. There didn't seem to be any allegiance to what Slim had always thought to be up there with Newton's laws – the sanctity of time, the holiness of the schedule. The farther out in the boonies and the shabbier the buses the less likely it was that there be any schedule at all. When is this bus leaving? Soon, very soon. An hour ago you said we were leaving soon. When do you think . . . ? Right away. Very soon. Slim rapidly figured out 'very soon' meant whenever every seat in the vehicle was taken, the roof racks were overloaded and roped down, and various ragged Indios were riding the bumper. Even spiffy modern buses you might catch in Mexico City and blow down the paved highway to Oaxaca would decide to depart more or less according to the whim of the driver, and once on the road untoward things would always happen.

But America was different, was it not? America ran on time. America was the land that said what it was going to do and stuck to its promise. Things were clean and efficient. Crazy stuff didn't happen like it does in Mexico. He was thinking of the time when he was drowsing in a front row bus seat through the night passing by Michoacán at 70mph, when there came a tremendous wake-up smash and Slim felt his ankles exposed above sandals sprayed in a warm mist. The bus had demolished a drowsing donkey overnighting on the warm tarmac and stove in its front end, so it was a while before it got light enough for Slim to see that his ankles had been sprayed not with oil or brake fluid or some other vital bus liquid, but with blood. Donkey blood. The tremendous force of the impact had vaporized the donkey and driven his blood right through the steel and plastic front end of the bus.

Slim was pretty sure they weren't going to clean out any donkeys off the interstates in Tennessee and Missouri but his faith in the sanctity of American ways and means had been shaken somewhat by Lt. Kilo-Watt dragging that young man and his pistol off the bus in Penn Station. So it was off across America riding the Greyhound and they were standing in Dallas with their precious boxes just about when the schedule predicted. But as for crossing the field of dreams in your streamlined stratocruiser trouble free and care less; that childhood 1950s vision of a flawless, frictionless America suffered a few more hard knocks.

The route west seemed to be divided into long hauls and locals so passengers were getting on and off all the time including one grizzled customer in Kentucky walking to the back of the bus carrying all his luggage – one paper bag. 100 miles later, the call came from the back that the man needed help. He was comatose and needed help to the extent that the driver grabbed his wrists and Slim held him by the ankles and they carried him off, set him on the ground next to his paper bag, and left him there.

The only window that opens in these buses is a small slider next to the driver which, when opened, has the Venturi effect of drawing interior air up to the front and out. Combine that effect with another of a toilet that had been accumulating for 24 hours by the time they hit the Mississippi, and a new driver female settling into place who zipped open the slide window, and they were being assaulted by nauseating effluvia coursing from the toilet up the aisle and out her little window. The hoi polloi in the seats began to tactfully suggest some other kind of arrangement but she came on as the toughest bitch ever to drive a big bus and paid them no heed. When it became apparent they might all pass out from effluvia poisoning, Slim thought of something he had noticed in the commode so he lurched back to take the law into his own hands. There was some sort of contusion manufactured into the outside wall of the tiny toilet compartment that was topped by lettering warning the public to keep hands off 'Danger!', etc., but Slim could see it actually masked a thin covering that seemed vulnerable. He balanced on one foot and slammed the heel of the other into the vulnerability. Lo and behold there appeared a 3" circle open to the outside which immediately summoned a vortex sucking the stench out and away.

Things didn't improve when the next driver, who took over in Arkansas, turned out to be a rookie and got himself all muddled up spinning round the back streets of Little Rock looking for the station. A muttering and grumbling started by a few hard cases crescendoed to the point where the driver, frustrated anyway by his own incompetence, pulled the bus over, yanked the emergency brake and strode back looking to challenge the dissenters. Nothing like a bus brawl to clear the head, especially since the driver was white, many of the complainers were black, and Little Rock was the site of an unholy and infamous race riot in 1954. So Slim thought to remind everyone that we were all sitting here and now in this bus hoping to get to the same place, weren't we? How about we calm down and get back on the highway.

O.K., back on track and booming through the middle of the night toward the Texas border, now Slim's 11 year old daughter got up out of her seat, walked the aisle to the front, stepped down, and tried to open the door going to that friendly place in dreamland before she woke. She wasn't a usual sleepwalker but one surmises the chaos and insecurity of life on the bus set her off to find her own place. But with the sunrise, a new dawn and a 75mph speed limit on the Texas plains, they were not long for Dallas. Standing in the lot stretching and yawning, their light bulbs dim, their wattage depleted, Slim thought even the magnetic NYC cop would have had a hard time keeping himself from sleepwalking right off that bus.

19

NO MAN'S LAND

When you're living on the land and living in Vermont and you're surrounded by maple trees, it's a sure bet you will be boiling maple syrup. That's what Slim figured and thusly had put together a conglomeration of used and abused pans, tanks, arches and grates. He knew you could make syrup with just a pot, a fire pit and many hours of sitting, stoking and watching but if you wished to get at least semi-serious and produce more than a mere gallon or two, you would need a traditional rig be it 6 or 12 or 16 feet long. A common syndrome among syrup makers is the desire for a bigger and/ or better rig. The dream is always more syrup produced in less time using less firewood. Consequently most folks are hardly ever satisfied with the rig they already have and are looking to trade up. So, when BobCap called to ask wouldn't he like to come along to help pick up a sap tank across the border in Québec, Slim wasn't surprised and readily agreed. Vermont is famous for its maple syrup and makes more than any other state in the U.S.A. but many Americans don't realize the maple capital of the world is the province of Québec in Canada. Québec produces vast quantities of syrup and involves thousands of people in its production. It is therefore fertile ground for the finding of used equipment, especially given the switch-over to all-stainless steel within the preceding 25 years.

They were riding BobCap's old pick-up and burning his gas. Slim was just along for the company and the muscle power to wrestle the tank on and off the truck. There would be no hassle crossing the border according to BobCap – no import-export taxes or fees – no tedious paperwork necessary – they wouldn't give a second glance at an old truck with a sap tank in the back. Slim lived a two hour drive south of the Canadian border and in the past had occasionally gone north to visit Montréal; on one occasion taking the family to an Expos game in the days when they still called Montréal home. On those trips, you would often go through the checkpoint with just a wave at and from the border agent Or he might stop you to ask a few polite questions before sending you on your way. Or at the very worst he might ask to see your driver's license, but Slim could not remember that ever happening. Those were the halcyon days. The days before 2001. The days before those Arabs shocked the country into a frenzied paranoia. The days before the border guards turned squinty-eyed suspicious, their very jobs on the line, the country depending on their perspicacity to keep the terror at bay.

But what did Slim know of all this? Oh yes, he certainly knew about the towers crashing and burning but his life was all sap and apples and firewood, and when they arrived at the Canadian border he was planning on waving and smiling and cruising on through to pick up that tank. The French-speaking customs officer checked BobCap's driver's license and then leaned in to look at Slim, saying, "Where's yours?" Who me? I'm just along for the ride. I didn't bring my license. I'm just here to help. "Like hell you are! What kind of joke is this? Turn right around and go back to where you came from. And don't try any funny stuff. I'm calling the other border stations to let them know about you."

Now let's picture the situation. As you drive north you first pass the U.S. customs building and checkpoint where they pay you no mind, then you proceed 100 yards to the Canadian checkpoint. In between is 100 deserted yards of two-lane highway – a veritable 'no man's land'. So when BobCap u-turned at the Canadian side and headed back through the American, having resolved to leave Slim somewhere downstream to hitch a ride home, and the U.S. customs man says, "Identification?" Slim began to stutter um, uh, um. Like a dope slap it suddenly hit him that as far as they were concerned here he was coming from Canada trying to enter the U.S. without the slightest shred of identification. Then the man, staring at Slim, asks, "Where were you born?" and he answers merrily: Bahrain.

One of the ironies of this story is that both of Slim's parents were Canadian and he was therefore a natural-born Canadian citizen who had just been refused entrance into Canada. It so happened they were in Bahrain working an oil refinery when Slim was born. In fact, they lived and worked in Bahrain for many years so Slim and his siblings had passed much of their childhood there. As far as Slim was concerned it had been an idyllic childhood, innocent as he was from any social or political concerns viz the resident Arabs. The American, Canadian and English employees of the oil company and their families lived in a newly constructed town surrounded by a serious fence with two gates, north and south. The fence was there to keep the Arabs out but conversely it allowed young Slim at least the illusion of total freedom, his parents, knowing their children to be fenced in, unconcerned about his whereabouts and doings.

When Slim told this story later to his father, the old man gave him this advice, "Don't tell them Bahrain. Just say Philadelphia or Albany or some place like that and they won't ask any more questions." However, at that time and that place he felt happy about being a kid in Bahrain and didn't think twice, up to the second after it came out and Mr. Customs Man performed a strange facial calisthenic then said quick and terse, "Get out of the truck." What the hell? thought Slim, and he began to babble loudly and at top speed as to how they hadn't been in Canada, hadn't in fact ever left the U.S., had just gone by five minutes ago, hadn't he seen them, the Canadians didn't let him in, they had to turn around.... Paying no mind to this obviously fabricated and pathetic bluster, and confronted with this sneaky Bahraini, Mr. Man's face now assumed the Mt. Rushmore affect of the rock-solid lawman saving his country from disaster and repeated his command: "'Get - out - of - the – truck."

BobCap turned around once again and motored off into Québec to get his sap tank, and they marched Slim into the building to decide upon his fate. "You got no identification.

Thinking you can sneak by us and get into the country illegal. What kind of knucklehead are you anyway? No way we're going to let you in. You just go back to where you came from." "But that's just about word for word what the Canadians told me. Listen here. I am a U.S. citizen. I did time in the U.S. Army. I live right here in Vermont. Back to where I came from is south of here 100 miles to the famous burg of South Washington, the center of the universe;" . . . and friend and sap tank and truck and Québec and on and on madly. The chief of staff began to pound at his computer. "What did you say your name was? You're not in here. You're not in the computer. If you're not in the computer you don't exist buddy. Maybe you should go back to Bahrain."

Slim could feel his gorge rising. He began to get testy with these perceived morons, later modified after the heat of battle to just government guys doing their jobs. "This is reminding me of something. Oh yeah – North Korea. It's the DMZ out there. I can't go that way and I can't come this way. I'm stuck in the middle. O.K., gentlemen, I see my only option is to set up a homestead in the DMZ. If you will be so kind as to lend me a pup-tent, I'll find a good spot out there. I can beg food from the north-south traffic, get water from your hose to drink and bathe – the passers-by will find that an invigorating sight – and generally become a tourist attraction. The people will talk about me begging food and coffee and an occasional beer – a little brewski now and again to liven things up – and the newspapers will come by to interview me as I will have become a cause célèbre." "Don't give us any of that French shit just because you've come from Québec and what is this happy horseshit about a pup tent?"

"All right boys, I'll tell you what you're going to do. To hell with your stupid computer – it obviously has only half a brain. Get on the phone and call the DMV in Montpelier. I live in Vermont and you all live in Vermont. We all drive cars so we're all registered at the DMV. Call them now and stop wasting everybody's time. Here's my name, my address and the name of my beautiful wife who is also on the registration. That should do it."

And it did. Slim walked away from the border with his thumb out and with the best wishes of the border boys: "Get the fuck out of here and don't let us see your ugly face again." He hitched to a friend where he phoned his beautiful wife who got on her pony and rode to the rescue. While waiting for the pony express he accompanied his friend, a dairy farmer, to check on the status of a corn plantation. Now, for the final irony, the friend looked left and right to check his location and said, "Welcome to Canada." Uncomprehending, Slim could only reply, "Wha?" The corn field ran south to north and on its upper end plowed and harrowed right across the border. So there he was, free as the breeze standing in Everyman's Land! And thus ended Slim's brush with myth and legend. Unlike Charlie riding the MTA, he who never returned, Slim had escaped his fate of being doomed to be forever stuck in No Man's Land.

20

ON THE EDGE

The truck was a 1950 six wheel GMC that had been tricked out for telephone and power line work. It had a winch and a boom that was bedded into a solid steel body so it could lift up to 10,000 lbs. It had side walls five feet high that were double decks of cabinets – ten to each side – cabinets that still held some of the tools of the trade and miscellaneous bolts and lengths of cable although there was no telling how long ago the truck had been retired from power line work. It had two eight inch hooks welded to the back to accommodate a supersized skid chain. It had a steel belaying post 12 inches high on which to snub a one inch manila rope to hold a pole upright. It had a swiveling head light on top of the cab for illuminating a night job. It was put together with a lot of thought and engineering for one sole purpose which unequivocally did not include cross-country travel. The truck came off the GM assembly line as a standard 2-ton Carryall and it came with a standard six cylinder engine. No manufacturer today would even contemplate powering such a big truck with such a small engine, plus when you add the extra thousands of pounds of steel put on to beef it up in support of the boom and winch, you have created a behemoth that would have trouble even maintaining the minimum posted speed on the interstate. The truck was a lumbering beast, seriously overweight and underpowered, but, undaunted, they had it on the highway looking to stretch it all 2,500 miles from Oregon to Vermont.

Old Slimshanks was along for the ride. He was riding shotgun and taking turns driving for his son, young Coggs. They were bound to propel this truck, if even by sheer willpower, all the way across the continent. Why they were doing this remains somewhat of a mystery. It's true the truck was a unique individual. It was highly unlikely that another one just like it existed in the whole of the U.S. of A. But that didn't appear to be a motivating force behind purchasing this monster of an ancient truck as far from home as possible thereby being left with the cowboy's task of herding the beast home. It was one of those affairs that happen in the realm of unreason and inevitability. It was just that young Coggs wanted that rig back home. He wanted it to lift heavy stone and he wasn't fazed by the buildup of fifty vehicles in a long grumpy line behind them once they crossed over onto the two-lane Trans-Canada Highway. The Canadians didn't exactly live up to their pleasant, mild-mannered reputation once they were able to blow by in an uphill passing lane, honking, fishtailing and throwing out the finger. Get the fuck off the road you tortoise of a Vermont truck. It had become a Vermont truck once they left Oregon when young Coggs tacked on a Green Mountain plate he had removed from some vehicle retired out in the home pasture. But the jog into Canada, in order to avoid the Detroit, Chicago, Cleveland, Buffalo conglomeration, was still a long drive and many harrowing days away, 1500 miles to the east on the other side of the mountains.

The Rocky Mountains and the Continental Divide lay before them and if they could just make it over they figured it to be downhill all the way at least to the Mississippi. They planned to follow Lewis and Clark in reverse: head out the Columbia; jog over to cross the Snake upstream of Hell's Canyon at Lewiston-Clarkston; cross the Idaho panhandle along the Clearwater; go over the Bitterroot Mountains at Lolo Pass; barrel down to Missoula then back over the Divide to Helena where they would part company with Lewis and Clark and head out onto the prairies. They soon learned the truck was a prodigious consumer of gasoline and while they were still feeling like 'Hallelujah, we're on the road', they were beside the road begging a ride to the nearest gas station.

Slim had always wondered when reading the accounts of Lewis and Clark how it was they didn't lose each other. They were continually making side trips off the river to investigate what was out there and they would say: I'll meet you upstream at such and such a place in so many days. Coming at it from a Vermont state of mind featuring endless heavily wooded tight valleys rendering any long distance reference points invisible, Slim couldn't fathom how they stayed in touch. However, now he could see – literally see – for 20 miles into the receding distances of this endless open country. Driving through eastern Oregon and central Montana, he could understand why people claim to become claustrophobic after moving to Vermont. The big sky is there all right but meanwhile the Rockies closed them in.

The first leg went fine – slow and steady up and over the Bitterroots through Lolo Pass grinding it out in second gear for 45 minutes then bowling downhill to Missoula, the brakes feeling okay. And they were feeling okay too. The old beast had surmounted the first obstacle, so now on to the Continental Divide which surely wouldn't be as steep as the run-up to Lolo. But it was. It seemed as if they were crawling up that mountain for most of the morning and by the time they were only half-way there were signs of trouble – an old car here and a pickup there were off the road with hoods up and radiators steaming. As the truck growled toward the top there appeared a sign, saying: You are approaching MacDonald Pass and the Continental Divide, el. 6920 feet, and Slim had a great idea. "Hey Coggs. Get Dr. Dan on the phone." Wha? Why? "We're going over the Great Divide. Let's bring him in. He'll love it." Dr. Dan the rig man was a powerful lover and restorer of old trucks and had taken great interest in this quixotic adventure, to the extent of recommending preferred routes and advising on how to motivate the old truck into action. "Hey Dan. It's Coggs. We're in the truck. We're booming up the mountain to the Continental Divide. We're almost there." Slim was driving. Put the phone on the floor against the front wall so he can hear. Right. They crested the mountain and what Slim wanted Dan to hear was the engine coming out of second gear and relaxing into third for the downhill run. They had been hammering along in low gear for an eternity and it seemed to Slim not only a physical and psychological relief to shift up but symbolic to them and Dan of an open road all the way home. "What the hell was that?" said Dan. "Is he shifting up? That damn fool! Tell that gear jamming, hot rodding idiot to DOWN SHIFT, DOWN SHIFT NOW!" Just then, as they started to pick up speed on the downhill run, there loomed ahead an enormous bright yellow sign spelling out in the largest black lettering Slim had ever seen on a road sign: STEEP GRADE. ALL TRUCKS USE LOW GEAR.

Oh! Shit! Slim's heart rate jumped up several hundred points as he declutched, pulled the shifter out of third and jammed it back into second. It gnashed and grimaced and didn't go. Slim figured force was the only option and smashed it up toward second gear. It would not go back in. They were going faster now. All right, third gear is better than nothing. He slammed it back into third. It wouldn't go in there either. They were stuck in neutral and racing down-hill into oblivion. The highway through MacDonald Pass on the way to Helena had been literally chopped, sliced or cut into the side of the mountain for several thousand feet of el-evation from top to bottom. Heading down on the passen-ger's side was nothing but air to make you dizzy looking over the edge, and on the driver's side was nothing but a rock wall marked by evidence of the dynamite and bulldozers used to chop into it. There was no hope – that is – there were the brakes and Slim stood on the pedal. They rounded one cor-ner, the truck holding steady, and came around another, the brakes already starting to feel woozy, when, by all that's holy in heaven, ahead was a scenic overlook jutting out over the chasm. They dove in at the top staying as close to the rail as possible, and, with everything he could put onto the brake pedal, followed the ellipse around until, just before rejoining the highway, the truck stopped. They jumped out. Thick smoke was pouring out of all four wheels. The brakes were fried.

Young Coggs hailed a transport vehicle from Helena which hauled them down the mountainside to spend several days twiddling their thumbs waiting for a new clutch. It turned out the old clutch didn't wish to cross the Divide and had shattered right there making it impossible to engage the transmission. While riding the tow-truck down, Slim pondered the vagaries of fate and luck. He felt rather more queasy than euphoric looking at the rock wall on one side, the chasm on the other, and contemplating the awful possibilities had that scenic overlook not been where it was. There was no apparent escape from mayhem and death that he could envision. The only chance he could see would have been to throw the truck against the rock wall and go downhill in a shower of sparks and shattered metal, but what would they have done to the many cars full of families coming up the other way?

It is not a disaster if it's a disaster averted. An inch is as good as a mile. Close doesn't count. Maybe it doesn't count to your still intact truck but to your fractured soul it surely does.

21

MISTER TREE

We named him Little Tree because we had just been reading a book out loud, 'The Education of Little Tree', and the kids had been enraptured. We, the adults, later learned the story that had been presented so vividly as real was actually fiction, but after a brief feeling of betrayal we came to think it didn't matter – the power and impact of the book carried all into its own realm of reality.

As he grew into his adult size and bearing, though still an adolescent, we felt it would be more dignified to call him mister – Mister Tree. Dignity however was not something he aspired to. If you didn't know him you might be taken in by his regal bearing, his handsomeness, and his black coat tinged with silver highlights. But from the beginning he was just a handsome and charming rogue.

The beginning took place at his birth home when we arrived in response to a neighborly tip. Just as we emerged from the car he came careening around the back corner of the house all by himself to greet us, a ball of fuzz wriggling with delight, tail wagging a windmill. There were five or six puppies in the litter and we religiously stuck to our plan of checking them all out but secretly we all knew – he had stolen our hearts and it was love at first sight. We had read about a sure-fire method of assessing a puppy's future personality. Put it on its back and hold it down with one hand on its chest. If it offers no resistance and does not struggle at all, that one will be a milquetoast with no strength of character. If it struggles mightily and does not give up, that one will be hard-headed and perhaps unmanageable. You want a puppy that will struggle for a while and then submit. The happy medium. The entire litter tested between one end and the other but it didn't matter, we were taking this lover boy home with us anyway. The How-to-Choose-a-Puppy paper didn't have anything to say about a puppy free of inhibitions, and issued no warning about a dog who loved humans too much. Not that it would have made any difference but the paper might at least have included a footnote.

It was a classic case of how do you keep them on the farm after they've seen Paree. It started one day when he didn't want to be left behind and followed the car to town. Town means people. People mean fun. Look at all these people! By this time Mister Tree had come into his handsome self. He was tall and long legged with a rich coat of black and silver hair and a magnificent plumed tail. And was he friendly! There was that person petting him and saying such a nice doggy; and this person scratching him behind the ears and telling him how beautiful he was; and yet another hugging him and bubbling baby talk and sweet nothings into his impressionable young ego. He figured he'd landed in heaven and from that time on Chelsea village became lodged in his brain as his own personal Mecca. His motto became why stay home and be bored when there would surely be a party going on somewhere else.

Mister Tree especially didn't appreciate being left behind when the whole family took off to go to, he was certain, a rollicking reveling party. To cement that belief in his world-view, he followed us one day. We left to attend a gathering at a nearby friend's telling Mister Tree to stay and guard the farm. It was a pleasant summer day so the party filled the living space and spilled over onto the deck. Everybody was drinking and yammering and enjoying themselves when Slim realized there was a dog in the crowd out there on the deck. It was Mister Tree! He was meeting and greeting and circulating and wagging that splendid plume of his – the life of the party. How did he get there? It was somewhat magical and mystifying. The distance measured 4 or 5 miles by road and 2 or 3 miles through the woods cross hill and dale but there he was, perhaps 45 minutes after us.

The event that sanctified his wanderlust – that left him in no doubt there was gold to be mined out there – came with a phone call. We have a dog here. I understand he might be yours. He had been gone for two days and the call came from a unit in a newly constructed low income housing complex in Chelsea. When Slim knocked on the door of #9 and a woman opened, he could see past her straight through a hallway to the back wall of the living room where a TV was set up exactly in line with his viewpoint. On the wall-to-wall arrayed in front of the TV, chins propped on their elbows, were three children and between them, chin lying on his forepaws, enthralled, was Mister Tree. She said he had been there overnight, the kids loved him and she'd gone to the store to buy the best canned dog food for him. Well, well, well. After that, compared to the prospect of sleeping in the woodshed and eating dry kibble, there was no keeping him home.

So we started tying him up. This is the last thing you ever want to do with a farm dog, and he agreed. He chewed through several ropes and dragged the remnants down to Chelsea. We moved up to chains: 25 foot light dog chains; then ¼" plastic-coated cable with end clips; then light duty farm chains; and finally a 12 foot 3/8" logging chain. Mister Tree dragged them all to Chelsea and some body or bodies collected them all. We never saw ropes or chains again and Slim had run through his entire repertoire. It was absurd – ludicrous even. What was the possible explanation for the dog's Houdini-like escapisms? He could certainly chew through rope and perhaps bend some flimsy end clips but obviously he wasn't going to chew through or break a length of chain, so . . . in the clarity afforded by a considered retrospective, it would appear the responsibility must rest with he who was doing the fastening. Slim would say to himself, this time I'm really fed up, I'm going to make sure he'll never escape again. But there must have been a little worm at work burrowing into his subconscious causing yet another hasty half-hitch or half-assed chain lock.

For Mister Tree's final act he disappeared for many days. We had received no news and were fed up so we decided not to look for him any more. A couple of weeks later a family friend dropped in to say she knew where he was. Oh? I've seen him in the yard of a little house on the highway on the other side of Chelsea. That house has been empty but just recently has been rented to a single man. His car has out-of-state plates. Slim called the man. He was recently divorced, had come to Vermont to rest and recover, and had brought his dog with him. Just after he'd moved into the tiny house by the road his dog was run over and killed, leaving him lonely and bereft. A few days later while driving home and approaching the house, he came upon this beautiful dog standing in the road. He stopped, talked to the dog who had no collar and asked him if he didn't want to jump in. The dog was happy to oblige and he loves him and they are the best of friends. Slim thought for not very long and quickly said, "It sounds like a match made in heaven. You know what? He's your dog now. You keep him."

We passed by the man's house some days later and noticed that his automobile was a classic Corvette convertible painted sky blue. The last time we ever saw Mister Tree we were standing on the library steps in downtown Chelsea when the sky blue Corvette with its throaty rumble and with its top down came cruising slowly up the main street. And there was Mister Tree sitting tall in the passenger seat so that the wind ruffled the top of his head, looking very proud like the true aristocrat he always thought himself to be, all the while monitoring the hoi polloi like a prince being chauffeured along the parade route.

{ **22** }

NASTY BOYS

When the American, British and Canadian oil men came in 1935, Bahrain was not exactly a sleepy little island. Bahrain had some history. It was undoubtedly the once mythical land of Dilmun where Gilgamesh sailed to in that oldest of the world's stories. It is home to a Portuguese fort constructed in the 16th century but now a crumbling tourist attraction. This fort was one of many which the Portuguese erected along their spice route around Africa and across the Indian Ocean to Goa. The island had long been famous for the pearls to be found off its shores. These were harvested by free divers who began their careers as small boys diving for silver coins tossed overboard by arriving visitors. Bahrain is only 30 miles long by 10 miles wide and situated between Iran and Saudi Arabia in the gulf called Persian by one and Arabian by the other. It has been favored beyond other neighbors in the desert climate with the one critical element – no, not crude oil but water, fresh water and lots of it. The water travels long distances underground from the mountains to the northwest in Saudi Arabia to surface as oases throughout the island. In some places just off shore, the water even wells up through the salt such that the water poor would row out into the ocean to dip their cans and come up with fresh water. The population is Arab and mostly Shia but the ruling dynasty, the Al Khalifa family who originally came down from Kuwait a couple of centuries ago, is Sunni. They had a good thing going in Bahrain and it got even better when the Americans arrived.

It was a sweet and quiet little island until ARAMCO (Arabian-American Oil Company) struck it big in Saudi Arabia. That's when the Al Khalifas realized they could get in on the bonanza and were happy to sign a deal with Standard Oil of California to build a refinery. The Americans teamed up with the British to form BAPCO (Bahrain Petroleum Company) and the rush was on.

Everything had to be brought in by ship and to start with there weren't even any wharves or docks so the ships had to unload onto dhows. The docks went in first and soon they had laid down roads. They built an airfield. They put together a refinery with its administrative buildings. They planned out and built a town to house the British, Canadian and American employees. They named the town Awali and the engineers had a field day designing and building a town from scratch. All the houses had flush toilets and were plumbed with Bahrain water, and distilled water from the refinery, and hot water from the refinery to provide heat in the winter. The houses were also hooked up to a central air conditioner which was a massive wooden tower filled with slatted floors through which water was cascaded and air was funneled then sent cooled out across the town. They built a club in which was consumed extraordinary quantities of beer. They built a swimming pool. They built tennis courts. They built a school for the children. They built a hospital. They leveled off a soccer pitch on which there was no grass. They even manufactured a golf course through the sand and rock by making 'greens' out of rolled oil-soaked sand and using balls painted red. The refinery and the golf course were a ways out of town but Awali itself and its accoutrements were all enclosed by a fence. The town was in the center of the island and was inside a fence with only two openings – a north and a south gate. The gates were monitored continuously and were closed at night. The fence was chain link and was perhaps six feet high and topped by several strands of barbed wire set out at an angle.

There were plenty of Arabs who worked at the refinery. These were paying jobs sought after by Bahraini men who were picked up every morning by a Bapco bus and taken back home in the evening. They were trained for specific jobs but most of them were considered to be 'coolies'- men who did the grunt work of hard physical labor. Some of the 'coolies' lived in palm-leaved shacks nearer to Awali and so walked home. In the cool of the winter, several would walk a shortcut across a 'lake' of tar on which had congealed a top crust. This tar was considered a waste product left over after the gasoline, kerosene, diesel, etc., was extracted from the crude and it was pumped while hot into a depression near the refinery to such an extent it formed a lake. One day a man leaving work got halfway across before the crust gave way and he began to sink into the viscous tar. It was worse than quicksand and as he struggled he continued to sink while they tried various strategies to save him. It was a slow sinking but in the end he finally submerged and disappeared into the tar. The man was an Arab and the unanswerable question remains: If he'd been an American, wouldn't some means, however drastic, have been found to save him?

The fence around Awali was the real thing. It was at least two miles long with only two gates and was there for one reason – to keep the Arabs out. There were Bahrainis who came into Awali during the day who were gardeners working for individual employees and there were also houseboys who cooked and cleaned for the wives or who bussed in the club. The houseboys and busboys were recruited from India and they and the Arab gardeners all left before nightfall when the gates would be closed.

Awali was where Old Slimshanks lived before he was old enough to earn his shanks, so we will call him Little Slim. Life in this artificial company town was a kind of paradise for Little Slim. The men were all at the refinery during the day and the women didn't worry about their children because they were fenced in. The mothers were also able to keep track since they were connected through a central telephone operator who would pass on updated location reports: "Little Slim is down on the drive headed for the South gate" – at which point Slim's mother would hop the bus which continuously circled the town to find and fetch him. Although, once, when he was five, she arrived to find him on the outside of the gate seated in the midst of group of Arabs chewing qat, babbling away and having a fine old time. Generally children wandered around Awali at will and there were plenty of them during the years of the 40s and 50s. BAPCO appreciated the virtues of married employees and encouraged them to bring their families with them during their stay in Bahrain.

Little Slim was of course oblivious to any politics surrounding the fence or the relations between whites and Arabs. His earliest hero was Hajji the gardener. He used to follow Hajji around, certain he held the key to unlock the answers to life's deepest mysteries. Hajji taught Little Slim how to brush his teeth. At the outside faucet he would sip some water then rub along his teeth upper and lower with his index finger, so Little Slim adopted the technique as the only true and real method of cleaning one's teeth. "I don't care what Hajji showed you," said his mother, but Little Slim would follow his guru. Once, from behind an oleander bush, he watched Hajji piss into a jar and that became a 'cause célèbre' for his parents when they began finding Little-Slim-stashed jars around the yard. Hajji was not his given name. That is an honorific only for a man who has made the pilgrimage to Mecca. Little Slim would often see him on his knees with his forehead on a square of cloth and had imitated him to start with but stopped because it was boring and his father explained it was something Hajji did but they didn't.

The majority of the refinery's employees housed in Awali were engineers, chemists, accountants and managerial types and they kept their own society playing bridge, alternating dinner parties and hosting square dances. But there was another group of men who were there on short-term contracts and were recruited from among the British working class. They were pipefitters, welders, automotive mechanics, plumbers and carpenters. Many of these were bachelors who became bored spending their nights drinking beer and brawling over other men's wives and so they left for home. But there were some who brought their families, and Little Slim had plenty of British brats for playmates. 'Brat' was not in his vocabulary at the time but he got a clue to its meaning when they were exploring an abandoned and crumbling loading dock. One of them had climbed to the top and called down to Little Slim to come over and look up through this hole left by a rotten plank. When Slim did so, the boy proceeded to piss all over him. Now, we all know the process of 'growing up' entails a certain creeping loss of idealism vis-a-vis our fellow humans but this was a rude awakening for Little Slim, and there were more to come compliments of these British brats. Little Slim was six or seven during these times and was a sponge for any cultural inflow. He knew the Arabs were different and could account for that, but for the ethical standards of behavior of white people to deviate so much from those of his own family was a big surprise.

The next incident took him over the fence and into the Arab desert. He and two English mates had figured out how to conquer the fence and climb over without being snagged on the barbed wire at the top. They had been regularly commuting to a 'fort' beyond the fence without the knowledge, at least, of his parents. It was a rocky declivity, a crease in the desert floor they had outfitted with purloined fort-

necessary supplies. They emerged from their crack in the desert one day to encounter to their amazement an Arab man standing there staring and accompanied by a herd of goats. He seemed perhaps more astonished to see them, three little white boys out there in Arab land, but, remembering his manners, he pulled out a tin cup from beneath his robe, poured water from a skin he had slung over his shoulder, and held it forward – a precious offering to the Sahib's children. The youngest boy, a six year old, yelled, "We don't want any of your filthy, stinking water!" and slammed the cup out of his hand onto the sand.

Horrified. Horrified and instantly terrified, Little Slim turned and bolted for the safety of the fence. The Brits followed and the three pelted across the stones and sand as if the very furies from hell were chasing. Little Slim was not old enough to gauge what might be going through the goatherd's mind just then but he knew something very wrong had happened It scared him to his core and he could not fathom how a such a small boy could be so insulting to anyone. However, his education-by-Brit-brat wasn't over yet and he was about to be led into the ultimate realm of high crimes and treason.

Awali had been so planned and plumbed that there was plenty of water available to maintain small gardens, some grass, acacia trees and lots of oleanders. There were oleanders everywhere in Awali. They are heat and drought adapted and cheerfully always smattered with flowers. As bushes or small trees they were often set as hedges defining the limits between one house and the next. Little Slim and yet another Brit brat, not one of the former, rounded the end of one oleander hedge into a secluded yard and in front of them was a gardener on his knees facing Mecca praying. He was facing away from the two boys. His head was down and his rear was up. The brat took two quick steps and kicked him full force in the rump.

Beyond horror; beyond terror; what Little Slim was feeling was mortification - a queasy sense of shame and humiliation. This gardener was not Hajji but it easily could have been and would have made no difference to the Brit with no sense. Just a little boy, knowing not how to make sense out of such vulgarity, Little Slim fled home in tears and, swallowing hard, never once said a word about it.

Bob Machin writes and homesteads in central
Vermont. He has spent plenty of time in Latin
America but now grows food for the family,
squeezes apples in his cider mill, and boils
maple syrup. He has authored a previous Vermont book, *At loose in the Puckerbrush*.